The Exceptional
Real Estate Agent

Because Competence *Gives You* Confidence...

Jennifer Allan-Hagedorn, GRI

Copyright 2017 © by Jennifer Allan-Hagedorn

All rights reserved

Bluegreen Books

publisher@bluegreenbooks.com

ISBN: 978-0-9899326-3-9

Edited by Barbara Munson, Munson Communications, www.munsoncommunications.com
Cover & interior design by Sheryl Evans, Evans Studios, www.evans-studios.com

No part of this book may be reproduced or utilized in any form by any means, electronic or mechanical, including photocopying and recording, or by any information storage and retrieval system, without the prior written permission of the copyright owner unless such copying is expressly permitted by federal copyright law.

The scanning, uploading and distribution of this book via the Internet or via any other means without the permission of the publisher is illegal and punishable by law. Please purchase only authorized electronic editions and do not participate in or encourage electronic piracy of copyrightable materials. Your support of the author's rights is appreciated.

NOTE: REALTOR® is a federally registered collective membership mark which identifies a real estate professional who is a Member of the NATIONAL ASSOCIATION OF REALTORS® and subscribes to its strict Code of Ethics.

Contents

Preface	iii
Introduction	1
Who Is the Best Real Estate Agent You Know?	1
What's So Great About Being Exceptional?	2
What You Will (Not) Find in This Book	4
About Me & About Selling with Soul (SWS)	4
Chapter 1	7
Are You on the Right Flight?	7
Who is the Best Agent You Know?	8
Are Real Estate Services a Commodity?	9
The Exceptional Agent Quiz	10
INTERLUDE: Infomercial & Disclosure	18
Chapter 2	19
What Does It Mean to Be Exceptional?	19
What Makes an Agent Exceptional?	20
JENNIFER'S BLOG: Nice is Nice, but Good is Better	22
Chapter 3	25
The Eight Attributes	25
Attribute #1 Market Mastery	26
JENNIFER'S BLOG: A Big SOI A-HA Moment!	35
Attribute #2 MLS Mastery	37
Attribute #3 Contract and Disclosure Mastery	41
INTERLUDE—Dates & Deadlines	44
Attribute #4 Pricing Expertise	47
INTERLUDE: Pricing by Price Per Square Foot (PSF)—PUH-LEAZE NO!	50
Attribute #5: Photography Skills	59
JENNIFER'S BLOG: Do You Disclose an Obvious Material Defect In Your Marketing?	70
Attribute #6: Good Problem-Solving and Negotiating Skills	74
JENNIFER'S BLOG: Before You Freak, Do the Math!	78
JENNIFER'S BLOG: Something Troubling You?	88
Attribute #7: A Great Team	89

Attribute #8: Great Systems in Place to Track Transactions	97
In Conclusion (of Part 1, that is)	**109**
Interlude	**110**
Welcome to Part II	**111**
Two Paths to Success	113
The 80/20 Agent Versus the 20/80 Agent	115
How About a 20/80 Plan?	117
How To Be a Real Estate Professional	118
Strategy #1: Prioritize Your Current Clients Over Your Future Ones	118
Strategy #2: Watch Your Language	118
Strategy #3: Advise, Don't Sell	120
Strategy #4: Be Honest—Would Your Marketing Work on YOU?	121
Strategy #5: Stop Negotiating Your Fee (but no, you don't have to charge everyone the same!)	122
Strategy #6: Don't Memorize Scripts, Have Conversations!	124
Strategy #7: Guide, Don't Push	126
One Final Rant Before We Conclude…	132
Conclusion	**133**
Do We Want to Change?	133
Let's Start with Easy	134
Onto the Not-So-Easy Path to Professionalism	134
But While We're on the Subject…How About a Salaried Real Estate Agent?	137
Higher Barriers to Entry?	140
JENNIFER'S BLOG: I'm Looking for a New Agent Training Program	142
APPENDIX	**145**
BONUS! Real Estate Consulting – What's it All About?	146
Is Real Estate Consulting Right For You? A Quiz to Find Out!	147
What's next?	152
Additional SWS Resources	153
More Books by Jennifer Allan-Hagedorn	153
SWS Course & Programs	153
The SWS Community	153
Sample Listing Under-Contract Checklist	154
Sample Active Listing Checklist	155
Sample Buyer-Under-Contract Checklist	156

Preface

Exceptional: ex·cep·tion·al Adjective
Unusually excellent; superior: *an exceptional violinist*

This book is about being Exceptional. Not average, not mediocre, not good-enough-for-government-work. Exceptional.

Exceptionally competent. Exceptionally responsive. Exceptionally knowledgeable. Exceptionally ethical. And yes, Exceptionally successful!

It's no secret the general public doesn't think much of the real estate industry and I can't say I blame them. Honestly, the ridiculousness preached as gospel in this industry at times is truly astonishing, and I don't mean that as a compliment.

Many surveys have been done over the years that, time and again, confirm the public's mistrust of the real estate ~~profession~~ industry and its practitioners. Time and again, we land down there at the *bottom* of the list of "most trusted professions" alongside stockbrokers, politicians and car salespeople.

Why? Oh, there are plenty of reasons, many of which will be discussed (or, better said, ranted about) throughout this book. The abysmal disregard of the importance of competence training for our new practitioners is one reason; the laughably low barrier to entry into the career is another. Toss in the pervasive attitude that real estate is a "sales career," plus the intelligence-insulting marketing commonly produced by our practitioners...and don't even get me started on our compensation structure that creates an indisputable conflict of interest between our need for a paycheck and our contractual obligations to our clients.

But, so what? What does it matter to the average real estate agent, who just wants to get up in the morning, go to the office and do what he's told to do without worrying about what the public thinks of what he's doing?

Well, maybe it doesn't matter to that average agent...

But does it matter to YOU?

If so, I invite you to join me on a mission. A mission to stop complaining about the real estate industry with its misplaced priorities and unprofessional behavior and incompetent practitioners...and actually do something about it.

Let's let the world in on what we already know—that there IS a better way to practice real estate; that there ARE real estate licensees out there who care about their clients and want to be the best thing to ever happen to them. And that a career in real estate CAN be an honorable profession to be proud of, not apologized for.

Let's let home-buyers and -sellers know that they don't have to hold their noses and reluctantly hire average real estate agents to incompetently represent them; no, they can hire EXCEPTIONAL ones and be delighted with their hiring decision.

Are you in?

Introduction
Who Is the Best Real Estate Agent You Know?
(This is a trick question!)

Quick, name the very best real estate agent you know! The one you consider to be the most knowledgeable, the most competent, the most ethical; the agent YOU'D be most likely to hire if you had a need for professional real estate services for yourself or a member of your family.

Do you have a name?

Well, I hope you know that the correct answer is…YOU! You are the best real estate agent you know! Or at least, if you aren't quite yet, it's in your business plan to get there as quickly as possible.

Yes? Well then, this book was written with you in mind. YOU, a real estate licensee who sees this not as a job but as a profession. A career where you CAN be Exceptional at what you do and change peoples' lives in the process. Where you can get up every morning proud of what you do because you do it well, with integrity, conviction and a commitment to excellence.

Blah blah blah…Okay, so that sounds all warm and fuzzy and cute and sparkly, but what does it mean in the real world? IS being an Exceptional Real Estate Agent™ something you even want to be?

Well, let's talk about that!

Being an Exceptional Real Estate Agent starts with a desire to be, well, Exceptional! But it goes deeper than just something you'd *really like to be*— it's something you're willing to invest time, energy and perhaps even a few dollars into becoming. Because as wonderful as you no doubt are, simply being a generally wonderful, ethical, hard-working person doesn't make you an Exceptional Real Estate Agent. Know why?

Because...a real estate transaction is complicated. Competently managing the exchange of real property between a buyer and a seller requires knowledge, expertise and an intimate understanding of the process.

But being a generally wonderful person sure doesn't hurt.☺

What's So Great About Being Exceptional?

Why might you want to be an Exceptional Real Estate Agent? The Best Real Estate Agent You Know? And while we're at it, why might being The Best Agent You Know also be the Best Thing You Can Do for Your Business?

Reason #1: Confidence

When you're great at what you do and you know you're great at what you do, the confidence that knowledge gives you will be apparent to others. You won't have to come up with a compelling elevator speech, hand out clever business cards or use magic trigger words or gestures to inspire people to trust you. No, the people you meet will be able to tell that you are capable of handling their (or their friends') real estate needs. No sales pitch required.

The confidence you have when you are Exceptionally good at what you do is a beautiful thing. And not just the confidence you exude when talking with potential clients, but also when you're simply chatting about real estate with friends, family and even the strangers you encounter in your day-to-day wanderings.

The subtle message that you believe yourself to be, *strike that*, that you KNOW you are an Exceptional Real Estate Agent is probably the most powerful prospecting you can do when out and about in the world—more effective than begging or bribing for business, memorizing scripts, dialogues and elevator speeches, or creating a super-duper glossy personal brochure. A humble air of confidence will inspire people to think of you as a real estate agent they'd trust with their business—and they'll very likely remember you.

So, where does this confidence come from? Does it come from reading self-help books about the power of positive thinking and reciting affirmations every morning about how awesome you are?

Um...no. While having a positive attitude about yourself probably won't hurt, it's not going to give you the confident air I'm talking about here. No, what will give you the confidence that you are an Exceptional Real Estate Agent is...of course... BEING an Exceptional Real Estate Agent!

Reason #2: Client Satisfaction = Referrals

When you're an Exceptional Real Estate Agent, your current clients will notice and they won't be able to keep their mouths shut about it—they will be singing your praises to anyone who will listen. When you do a great job for one person, they almost can't help but tell others about you—and the more happy past clients you have in your database, the more happy future clients you're likely to have in your database!

I know it can feel overwhelming to look at the sheer number of real estate agents in your market who are all competing for their share of a limited pie of home-buyers and -sellers, but rest assured that the vast majority of your competition provides, sadly, average, mediocre, just-good-enough-for-government-work service. Sure, some of them may have a marketing budget to die for, sending out thousands of mailers every month, taking out expensive ads in the local real estate magazine or paying big bucks for an Internet pay-per-click campaign, but you know what? The reason a lot of these agents choose to spend their marketing dollars this way is because they don't get the repeat and referred business that an Exceptional Agent would get, so they have to continue to pursue strangers for business throughout their careers!

(Of course, this is a generalization and if your business model includes spending a lot of money on advertising AND you enjoy a robust repeat and referral business, I'm not talking about you ☺.)

But please be assured that when your clients are thrilled with the service they receive from you, they WILL spread the word of your wonderfulness far and wide.

Reason #3: More Closings!

The third reason you might want to strive to be an Exceptional Agent is a very practical one. More paydays. Exceptional Real Estate Agents enjoy more visits to the closing table because they know how to get the job done. They know how to put and hold together real estate transactions. Their contracts don't fall apart when things get sticky because:

1. They're keeping a close eye on things as opposed to chasing after new business, and they know what to do to solve those potentially deal-killing challenges that inevitably arise during the contract-to-closing period.

2. When your job is to facilitate the exchange of real estate and you get paid when you are successful in your job, then guess what? The better you are at your job the more often you get paid.

It seems as if the real estate community forgets that we bring actual value to the process above and beyond simply being nice and friendly in hopes of generating more business. No, when we do an Exceptional job, not only do we generate future business, we also stand a much better chance of being paid for the business we're working on today.

So, yes, it's great if your buyers and sellers love you and think of you as a friend, but part of being the Best Agent You Know is producing the desired outcome. Results.

Which takes us back to that first reason to want to be Exceptional—when you know you know how to do your job well...that you know how to help a seller sell or a buyer buy and achieve an outcome they're happy with—talk about exuding confidence when you're talking to people about real estate.

And the cycle repeats. Sweet, huh?

What You Will (Not) Find in This Book

First and foremost...what you will NOT find in this book is much ado about prospecting. Oh, we may mention it from time to time in passing, but if you purchased this book hoping for tips and strategies to build your business from a gettin' clients perspective, you bought the wrong book. The right book, by the way, might be *Prospect with Soul for Real Estate Agents* ☺ also by yours truly.

What you will find in this book is both the motivation to Go Forth and Be Exceptional and details on how to do just that.

You'll also find random rants scattered throughout the book, mostly about the ridiculousness of some of the sacred cows of our industry.

In Part 2 of *The Exceptional Real Estate Agent*, you'll read about various strategies to enhance the professionalism of our industry, both as we appear to the general public and as we behave when with our fellow practitioners.

About Me & About Selling with Soul (SWS)

My guess is that you already "know" me—you found your way to this book because you've already read one or two or more of my previous six, or you've followed my blog or attended my monthly teleseminars. But just in case you stumbled onto *The Exceptional Real Estate Agent* by accident and have no idea who the voice is behind the words you're reading, here's a little bio on me (borrowed with revisions from my second book, *The More Fun You Have Selling Real Estate, the More Real Estate You Will Sell*).

I've had a real estate license since 1996 and practiced primarily in the Denver, Colorado area. I ran a good business and made a lot of money doing it. I worked under several brokerages and owned my own real estate company for a period of time.

I was a "real" real estate agent. As in...I wasn't some mega-producing superstar in a blue suit with a million-watt smile and an ego the size of Montana. I made mistakes and am not embarrassed to tell you about them. I was fired by clients, sometimes even deservedly so, and I dropped the ball on occasion. I showed up at the wrong title company for a contentious closing; I mis-measured houses, I offended prospects with politically incorrect jokes.

But I was also a Very Good real estate agent. I was successful by just about anyone's definition of success and I believe I made more people happy than unhappy over the course of my career. I pulled off miracles and changed people's lives.

Something else you should know about me—I'm not really a people-person. I'm not anti-social, just uncomfortable making small talk with strangers. I don't enjoy parties (the best I can say is that I tolerate them) and I often lost sleep the night before I met a new client worrying about the stupid things I might say to him during any awkward silences. While I rarely doubted my own competence and professional value, I almost always doubted my ability to carry on a decent conversation and build that oh-so critical rapport with a new buyer or seller.

I've started fresh...and burned out. Retired...and came back blazing. I've hired an assistant, fired an assistant, and even was an assistant. I owned a home-staging company and I owned a real estate company. I've worked sixty hours a week...and worked sixty hours a month. Been rich, been broke. Loved my job, occasionally hated my job. But throughout the fluctuations of my real estate career, the one thing that has never varied (okay, this is going to sound really sappy) is a commitment to serving my clients to the best of my ability. Seriously.

***

I am now a writer for the real estate industry. I've written six books (well, if you're reading this, I've now written seven) and have created a dozen or two training programs ranging from running a sphere of influence-based business to creating a real estate consulting practice. You can read more at my website www.SellwithSoul.com.

"Selling with Soul?"

So, speaking of, what's all this "Soul" stuff about?

Well, the textbook definition of Sell with Soul—at least the definition on the cover of the book and on the website is:

> *To enjoy a wildly successful career selling real estate by treating clients and prospects respectfully, as you yourself would like to be treated.*

Sound a little like the good old golden rule, doesn't it? Do unto others as you'd have them do unto you?

Well, that's intentional and there's certainly nothing wrong with a little golden rule in your real estate career, right?

But what does it MEAN exactly—to do unto others as you'd have them do unto you—as a real estate agent?

Well, to our way of thinking around here, it simply means that you provide a level of service to your clients that you would be satisfied with if you were the client being served by a real estate agent. Thrilled with, even.

And that's what this book is about.

Chapter 1

Are You on the Right Flight?

> *"Ladies and gentlemen, thank you for choosing our airline today. Our flight will take us to Dallas (or Detroit or San Francisco), so if going to Dallas (or Detroit or San Francisco) was not in your travel plans, please gather your things and make your way toward the exit."*

Ha ha ha.

Actually, I always do laugh a little at the joke, even though I've heard it a dozen times.

But seriously, here's the thing. The approach I'm about to share with you is different from just about any other out there, and if it isn't right for you, you are on the wrong "flight."

The Exceptional Agent philosophy attracts a small subset of the real estate community: real estate licensees who believe a career in real estate can and should be an honorable profession—one to be proud of, not apologized for. A career where members of the community believe that competently and compassionately serving our current clients is our first priority, that the buyers and sellers who have honored us with their business deserve our full attention and respect, and that any prospecting that needs doing can be done AFTER our current clients are taken care of. Members of the Exceptional Agent community naturally and intuitively run their businesses as professionals, not as salespeople, and are committed to being competent, even Exceptional Real Estate Agents who never take the business of their buyers and sellers for granted.

Does this sound like the right place for you? Not sure yet? Keep reading!

Who is the Best Agent You Know? (Of course, you now know that the correct answer is YOU).

But let's get more specific—what does being the Best Agent You Know entail? What, specifically, would inspire you to think of someone as an agent you would be willing to hire to represent you or someone you love?

Well, a few years ago I posed this question to my readership. I asked them what specific characteristics a real estate agent might bring to the table that would inspire them to think of the agent as someone worthy of their own business and/or referrals.

Here was one interesting response I received (paraphrased):

> *This is a difficult question to answer. You are likely offering much the same as any agent out there, so what sets you apart and how do you convey that to a potential client in a relatively short period of time? Other than the tools that most of us have access to and employ in one way or another, it comes down to personality and the rapport you build with a potential client. I think you just have to be a decent human being when dealing with your clients.*

Wow.

How do you feel about this? Do you agree that to be the Best Agent You Know, or even just reasonably refer-worthy, you simply need to be a decent human being who has a good personality and the ability to build rapport with your clients? Do you believe that what you offer your clients is pretty much the same as what every other agent offers, so it mostly comes down to having a pleasing personality?

Say it isn't so!

Obviously, I disagree with my reader's comments. But I was surprised, as more responses came rolling in, how many agents felt the same way. While no one else put it so bluntly, the majority of the responses ran along the same lines. The most-mentioned qualities had little to do with competence and a lot to do with personality. Many responders mentioned that they'd want an agent with good listening skills and empathy for their situation. Someone who wouldn't talk down to them, who would be patient with them, who would communicate with them on a regular basis; one who would show up on time and be responsive.

I wasn't sure how to feel about this. On one hand, I was pleased that so many of my readers mentioned what I'll summarize as "having compassion" as a critical characteristic of a great agent—after all, that's certainly not one of the traits that is celebrated in traditional real estate training. And I often feel I'm fighting an uphill battle when I teach and preach in public forums about the need for us to be respectful, patient, kind and empathetic with our clients as opposed to being pushy, aggressive, impatient and self-centered.

So, yes, I was delighted at the number of responses I received about being *compassionate* in their work.

But what surprised me was how few mentioned competency—those qualities of an agent that can mean the difference between the success or failure of a home sale or purchase adventure.

As I thought more about this (and believe me, I thought A LOT about it) I wondered if the lack of focus on the importance of competency is because the real estate industry as a whole doesn't place a lot of importance on being a *good manager of a real estate transaction* and we individual practitioners have bought into that.

Stay with me here as I overthink this...

Are Real Estate Services a Commodity?

Something I see and hear every day from agents—particularly newer ones—is a concern about what they bring to the table—what makes them special—what makes them better than their competition? And what, specifically, do they have to offer a buyer or a seller that would inspire that buyer or seller to choose them over someone else?

They seem to feel that the service they provide as real estate agents *is* simply a commodity and there's no real way to stand out from the crowd because what one agent can do for a client is pretty much the same thing another agent can do. That the only way to persuade someone to choose to work with you over someone else has to with personality and salesmanship, or maybe employing those gimmicks you've heard about to make someone trust you by the words you use or the gestures you make. Or, of course, to be the lowest bidder on your fee.

But you know what? There's something so much more compelling and valuable you can bring to the table that has nothing at all to do with a good personality or great salesmanship or clever gimmicks or even a commission reduction!

What might that be?

Competence

Simple. It's competence. Knowing your stuff and knowing you know your stuff. Yes, people skills are important, but without competence to back up those skills, you'll never be the Best Agent You Know. You may do okay—in fact, I believe a lot of real estate agents survive mostly on their people skills, but as likeable as they may be, as empathetic and patient and responsive as they are…if they don't know how to manage a real estate transaction from start to finish above and beyond the basics, they'll never be Exceptional Agents.

And this is very good news! Frankly, not all of us have a great personality—and I include myself in there! If my career were dependent upon people liking me enough to give me business, I'd have crashed and burned years ago. In fact, my biggest client used to say, "She's not the friendliest person in the world, but she gets the job done," and believe me, he was a big fan of mine if his referral patterns were any indication.

But if you are blessed with a decent personality AND a high level of competence, and let's throw in a good work ethic and some common sense…there's nothing in the world stopping you from being an Exceptional Agent and enjoying an extremely successful career that you're proud to call your own.

So, what's my point?

I want you to set a goal for yourself to be the Best Agent You Know within a year. Sooner, of course, is fine. But, starting today, I want you to begin working toward being the Best Agent You Know and, yes, that may take some time. You can't just go out this afternoon and create a great team or master your market or become a great photographer. But you can start putting the pieces and parts into place to make these things happen, if you're committed to making them happen.

Let's begin…

The Exceptional Agent Quiz

First, see where you stand now. *Is* The Exceptional Agent right for you? Let's find out. Following are some questions related to how you view a real estate career and your role in it. Go ahead and answer the questions honestly…and we'll see you on the other side ☺.

As a real estate licensee, I am first and foremost a salesperson and my primary job is to generate leads.

A) I agree with this statement. Most of the work done after the buyer or seller has hired me is best handled by my assistant so I can continue to focus on prospecting.

B) I disagree with this statement. My primary job as a real estate licensee is to use my expertise to help my clients manage their real estate transactions. Yes, I need to find clients to serve, but that doesn't make me a salesperson.

When I meet with a seller prospect, my primary goal is to get the listing agreement signed.

A) I agree 100%. That's why I go on listing appointments, to get the listing! Duh!

B) I disagree. When I meet with a potential seller, my goal is to help her determine if selling is the right thing for her to do at this time and if so, if I'm the right person for the job. I consider a listing appointment to be a fact-finding mission, not an opportunity to sell.

I am a competent, knowledgeable, ethical and hardworking real estate professional and I care deeply about serving my clients to the best of my ability.

A) I agree 100%! I'm not perfect, but I'd sure like to be. My goal is to be the best real estate professional I know!

B) I disagree. This is just a job to me and as long as it pays the bills, I really don't care all that much about whether or not I'm Exceptional at what I do.

A real estate agent who just got out of real estate school is ready to work with buyers and sellers and should begin prospecting for them right away. After all, the only way to learn is to DO, so the quicker a new agent has real clients to practice on, the quicker he or she will become competent.

A) Yes, I agree with this statement. New agents need to get out there and start learning the business and the best way to do that is to practice on real buyers and sellers.

B) No, I disagree. It is inappropriate and unprofessional for a new agent to use her clients to teach her how to do her job.

It's fine to take an overpriced listing because it will generate calls from buyers that I can convert into clients and sell them something else.

A) I disagree. Misleading a client as to the marketability of his or her property is unethical, especially if my goal is to "use" that client's unmarketable property to generate business for myself.

B) I agree with this statement. I need buyers, so I'll take any listing I can get, regardless of whether or not I think I can sell it.

When a listing isn't selling, the best solution is to reduce the price until it does.

A) I agree. Price cures all. Reduce the price enough, and the house will sell.

B) I disagree. While it may be true that a price reduction will sell the home, it's not always the best solution for the situation. It's our job as professionals to explore all solutions above and beyond a price reduction. In many cases, there is a better solution than simply adjusting the price.

You are in a coaching program that encourages you to prospect at least three hours a day, from 9am to noon. On Tuesday, you sit down to prospect and your phone rings. You see on your caller ID that it's your client with whom you have a closing at 4pm today. Do you:

A) Let it go to voicemail and call him back at noon?

B) Answer the call?

So, how did you do? Let's see!

As a real estate licensee, I am first and foremost a salesperson and my primary job is to generate leads.

A) I agree with this statement. Most of the work done after the buyer or seller has hired me is best handled by my assistant so I can continue to focus on prospecting.

B) I disagree with this statement. My primary job as a real estate licensee is to use my expertise to help my clients manage their real estate transactions. Yes, I need to find clients to serve, but that doesn't make me a "salesperson."

Correct Answer: B

Here at the Exceptional Agent, we strongly believe that a career in real estate is not a sales career. We agents are hired to manage the moving pieces and parts of a complicated process, and our clients trust us to place their current needs for competent service higher on our priority list than any needs we may have to find our future clients. Yes, as self-employed independent contractors we must always be looking for clients to serve, no different from any other self-employed person, but that doesn't make us salespeople.

However, confusion can arise due to the very real conflict that traditionally, real estate practitioners are paid on commission, and we are paid only when we "sell" something (i.e., real property). If we had no fiduciary duties to our clients, if we had no obligation to look out for their best interests, then perhaps calling ourselves salespeople would be appropriate.

However, real estate "sales" is different from virtually every other kind of sales because it requires us to accept fiduciary responsibility. We are expected to offer our clients our expert guidance, focusing on what is in that client's best interest, even when that advice is clearly not in our own. Can any of us say with absolute certainty that we've never recommended that a seller ask a price for their home higher than we believed it could sell for because we really wanted the listing? Even if we could say, with absolute certainty, that we've never done such a thing, is it possible our opinion of "value" was not even a little bit influenced by the fact that we wanted that listing, hoped we could sell that listing and needed the income that listing would likely generate? Our emotions can cloud our perceptions—it's basic human nature.

The consumer understands this. Has a buyer ever said to you, "How can you be trying to get the home for the lowest price when the more I pay, the higher your commission check?" Or how about the seller saying, "You only recommended that price to me because you want it to sell faster so you can get paid." Even when we are doing our very best for our client's best interest, they often question our motives, with good reason.

When I meet with a seller prospect, my primary goal is to get the listing agreement signed.

A) I agree 100%. That's why I go on listing appointments, to get the listing! Duh!

B) I disagree. When I meet with a potential seller, my goal is to help her determine if selling is the right thing for her to do at this time and, if so, if I'm the right person for the job. I consider a listing appointment to be a fact-finding mission, not an opportunity to sell.

Correct Answer: B

The idea that you meet with a potential seller for the sole purpose of getting a listing agreement signed is much more of a salesperson's approach than a professional's. And frankly, if a real estate licensee views her career as primarily a sales career, then this approach is right in line with her business model. However, a professional's mindset is that every meeting with a potential client is a MUTUAL interview to see if the relationship is one worth pursuing (for both). And when a professional talks with a homeowner, she does so with the goal of helping the homeowner evaluate his options in the current market to determine the best direction for him to take, which may or may not be to list his house.

I am a competent, knowledgeable, ethical and hardworking real estate professional and I care deeply about serving my clients to the best of my ability.

A) I agree 100%! I'm not perfect, but I'd sure like to be. My goal is to be the best real estate professional I know!

B) I disagree. This is just a job to me and as long as it pays the bills, I really don't care all that much about whether or not I'm Exceptional at what I do.

Correct Answer: A

Here at the Exceptional Agent, we're pretty proud of the fact that our community takes a real estate career seriously and wants to be the very best we can be. And that's the sort of professional we hope to attract more of.

A real estate agent who just got out of real estate school is ready to work with buyers and sellers and should begin prospecting for them right away. After all, the only way to learn is to DO, so the quicker a new agent has real clients to practice on, the quicker he or she will become competent.

A) Yes, I agree with this statement. New agents need to get out there and start learning the business and the best way to do that is to practice on real buyers and sellers.

B) No, I disagree. It is inappropriate and unprofessional for a new agent to use her first clients to teach her how to do her job.

Correct Answer: B

We feel pretty strongly that new agents have no business working with buyers or sellers until they are reasonably competent to do so. Why do we say this?

1. It's unprofessional (and bordering on unethical) to represent yourself as a competent real estate practitioner if you are not. Simple as that. Real estate school does not teach you how to manage a real estate transaction; it teaches you (primarily) how to pass the state exam.

2. If you take on clients before you are prepared to do so, those early clients will suffer from your inexperience...and they won't be quiet about it. They'll tell

everyone they know how clueless and incompetent you are, which is definitely NOT good for your future business.

Now, we're not asking you to wait months and months before pursuing clients. But show your career the respect it deserves and spend some time in the beginning building a solid foundation. You'll be glad you did.

It's fine to take an overpriced listing because it will generate calls from buyers that I can convert into clients and sell them something else.

A) I disagree. Misleading a client as to the marketability of his or her property is unethical, especially if my goal is to "use" that client's unmarketable property to generate business for myself.

B) I agree with this statement. I need buyers, so I'll take any listing I can get, regardless of whether or not I think I can sell it.

Correct Answer: A

To elaborate on this discussion item, here is an excerpt from my first book, *Sell with Soul*:

Is it Okay to Take an Overpriced Listing so You Can Acquire Buyer Leads?
No! It's not okay to take an overpriced listing just so you can acquire leads. We were not granted a real estate license by our state's real estate division so we could master the art of lead generation; we are licensed so that we can professionally assist the public with their real estate needs.

Page one of the Code of Ethics and Standards of Practice of the National Association of Realtors® actually states pretty darn clearly that: "Realtors®, in attempting to secure a listing, shall not deliberately mislead the owner as to market value." So someone thinks it's pretty important! We are not For Sale Signs For Hire; we are supposedly professionals who have more knowledge and expertise than our clients and should be trusted to share that knowledge with them.

Besides, don't kid yourself. Once your sign goes in that yard with a too high price, it will be All Your Fault when it doesn't sell. It doesn't matter how many disclosures you made or how much money you got up front for advertising, your seller will blame you when the home doesn't sell.

It's easy to forget this. To forget that we are hired by sellers to do a job, part of which might include telling them something they don't want to hear. In my opinion (and the opinion of your real estate commission), misleading a seller with respect to the marketability of her home is unethical. Ignorance of the market is no excuse. If you don't know (and are not willing to learn) the nuances of a particular market, you have no business going on that listing appointment. Real estate is not about you and your needs! Don't forget this!

Agents who take overpriced listings do a huge disservice to their clients—who they have committed (in writing on a legal document) to look out for.

Pricing listings right is an art and a skill that, once mastered, will make your life as a real estate agent much more pleasant, productive and profitable. All of us have taken overpriced listings and most of us swore we'd never do it again. But of course we do.

However, to take a listing you know is overpriced simply to get leads is in violation of your duty to your seller.

When a listing isn't selling, the best solution is to reduce the price until it does.

A) I agree. Price cures all. Reduce the price enough, and the house will sell.

B) I disagree. While it may be true that a price reduction will sell the home, it's not always the best solution for the situation. It's our job as professionals to explore all solutions above and beyond a price reduction. In many cases, there is a better solution than simply adjusting the price.

Correct Answer: B

Read the following excerpt from *The More Fun You Have Selling Real Estate, the More Real Estate You Will Sell*:

When Your Listing Isn't Selling, What's the First Thing to Fix? All Together, now...

PRICE!

Right?

Nope. Not always. Not even most of the time.

Many real estate agents claim that price cures all. And in a way, they're right. If you have a listing that shows poorly or is difficult to show or smells funny, there probably IS a price that will inspire buyers to overlook the clutter, access issues or eau de Chef Boyardee.

But is price the RIGHT answer? Again, not always. Not even most of the time[1].

---

[1] Unless you're overpriced to begin with, of course.

Why on earth not?

Three reasons.

First, I hope that when we real estate agents price our listings, we feel pretty good about that price. If I've put a price on a property, unless the market has declined, I'm pretty sure I'm in the ballpark.

Second, automatically resorting to the solution of reducing the price is really not what my seller wants to hear, and in that mindset, he's likely to question my professionalism and commitment. Let's face it, a price reduction is an awfully easy solution to offer and often abused by the real estate community. We all know agents who "buy" listings at a too-high price and then, as part of their game plan, beat up the seller later for a price reduction. So, when your first and only solution is a price reduction, I believe it can really damage your credibility, especially if you recommended or agreed to the price in the first place.

But third, and the main reason I'm opposed to looking first at the price as the solution is because it's rarely the best solution for the seller.

The thing is, there are tons of solvable problems—some simple, some not-so— that can keep an otherwise marketable home from moving. Our job is to play detective with our non-selling listings to determine if there's a problem we and/ or our seller can solve, outside of a price reduction.

You are in a coaching program that encourages you to prospect at least three hours a day, from 9am to noon. On Tuesday, you sit down to prospect and your phone rings. You see on your caller ID that it's your client with whom you have a closing at 4pm today. Do you:

A) Let it go to voicemail and call him back at noon?

B) Answer the call?

Correct Answer: B

The day a real estate professional chooses prospecting to strangers over taking care of her current clients is a grim day indeed. Enough said.

***

INTERLUDE:
Infomercial & Disclosure

I will mention this once and promise it shall not be spoken of again (at least not in this book).

As of this writing, a paid program is available called The Exceptional Agent Certification, which takes many of the concepts presented in this book and puts them into action. So, if you find you really like what you're about to read and would like to incorporate being Exceptional into your own real estate practice... and would like some additional guidance along the way, check it out.

www.TheExceptionalAgent.com.

Okay, infomercial over. Back to our regularly scheduled program.

Chapter 2
What Does It Mean to Be Exceptional?

An Exceptional Real Estate Agent is a real estate licensee who knows what the heck she's doing—and is committed to doing it well—very well. Perhaps even better than anyone else in town. Seriously. In fact, one of the goals we believe every Exceptional Real Estate Agent should have is to be the "best real estate agent I can be, perhaps even the best real estate agent I know."

To review from our Introduction, why might you want to make that your goal, too?

Reason #1
Confidence. When you're great at what you do and you know you're great at what you do, that confidence will be apparent to others. You won't have to come up with a compelling elevator speech, hand out clever business cards or use magic trigger words or gestures to inspire people to trust you; the people you meet will be able to tell that you are capable of handling their (or their friends') real estate needs. No sales pitch required.

Reason #2
When you're a great real estate agent, your current clients will notice—and they won't be able to keep their mouths shut about it! They will be singing your praises to anyone who will listen! Unfortunately, the bar in our industry is set rather low in the customer satisfaction department, so if YOUR clients are satisfied and they talk nicely about you behind your back, referrals will come. I promise.

Reason #3

The third reason you might want to strive to be an Exceptional agent is a very practical one. More paydays. Exceptional real estate agents enjoy more visits to the closing table because they know how to get the job done. They know how to put and hold real estate transactions together! Their contracts don't fall apart when things get sticky because:

1) they're keeping a close eye on things as opposed to chasing after new business, and

2) they know what to do to solve those potentially deal-killing challenges that inevitably arise during the contract-to-closing period.

But what does it mean to "know what the heck you're doing" as a real estate agent? WHAT, exactly, do you know how to do well—very well? Oh, we'll get to that ☺.

What Makes an Agent Exceptional?

If you were to ask a dozen real estate buyers or sellers what attributes they believe would make a real estate agent "Exceptional," you'd likely get at least two dozen different answers. But since this is my book ☺ I'll share with you what I believe those attributes (skills, services and masteries) to be, from a consumer's perspective:

1. Market Mastery—an Exceptional Agent understands and is "conversationally familiar" with the nuances of the local real estate market.

2. MLS Mastery—an Exceptional Agent is an expert in the local Multiple Listing System.

3. Contract and Disclosure Mastery—Exceptional Agents understand and can explain each and every provision in the contracts and disclosures they present.

4. Pricing Expertise—an Exceptional Agent understands how location, condition, features and amenities (or lack thereof) affect the value of the properties in their market area.

5. Photography Skills (or willingness to hire a photographer)—an Exceptional Agent understands the importance of having great photos online and is willing to invest the time and money to either take great photos himself, or hire someone to do it.

6. Good Problem-Solving and Negotiating Skills—an Exceptional Agent doesn't

fall apart and go all drama-queen (or king) when the going gets a little rocky. She stays calm and focused, and tackles the problem head-on. She is a skilled, confident negotiator.

7. A Great Team—an Exceptional Agent has a great team. If a client needs a referral to a handyman, house-cleaner, structural contractor, roofer or painter, an Exceptional Agent knows who to call.

8. Great Systems in Place to Track Transactions—Exceptional Agents have detailed checklists and follow-ups in place so that things don't slip through the cracks during their client transactions.

***

Reading through this list, did you notice that none of the eight attributes have anything to do with being nice, friendly, likeable or empathetic? Nothing really related to "people skills" (e.g., being a good listener) or what I call "compassion factors"?

Good catch! But there's a reason I exclude people skills/compassion factors from my list. It's not that I think real estate agents should strive to be a$$holes with atrocious bedside manners, of course, but rather because what we do, if we do it right, requires a fairly high level of competence, expertise and good old-fashioned hard WORK to properly serve the clients who have honored us with their business.

Being nice, likeable, friendly and empathetic isn't enough. It's just not. Yes, maybe having great people skills gets you in the door, but if you don't have the knowledge and expertise to get the job done that you were hired to do, all the people skills in the world aren't going to change the fact that:

1) your client is going to be disappointed and may very well share that disappointment with anyone who will listen; and

2) if you're paid on a contingent commission basis and can't get the job done, no payday cometh for you!

It takes more than a million-dollar smile, a firm handshake and a sympathetic ear to properly serve your clients. If you don't believe that, then I'll go out on a limb and say that your clients aren't being properly served, and I promise you, they notice. Oh, they may still like you personally, but inside, they're wishing they'd hired that other guy or gal who "...isn't the friendliest person in the world, but gets the job done."

JENNIFER'S BLOG: Nice is Nice, but Good is Better

Last month, I stopped by my bank to make a minor change to my business account. The gal who helped me was Nice, Really Nice. Friendly, chatty, made good eye contact and seemed truly interested in making sure I had a great experience in her bank that day. I left thinking lots of warm thoughts about her and my bank. She was Really Nice.

I emailed her the next day with a question about the change we'd made to my account. No response. I called and left a voice mail. No call-back. Called again. No call-back, again.

A few days later I tried to use the account we'd made the change to and something was wrong. It wasn't "working" right. I stopped by the bank for help. She identified the error she'd made and corrected it. Or so I thought. Actually, she corrected one mistake but created another.

I've now been in the bank four times and spent at least three hours with three different bankers trying to get my bank account to "work." All of them were Really Nice and I left the bank thinking all was going to be well.

Not sure if it is, indeed, "all well" yet, but I'm hopeful.

Anyway, here's my point.

When it comes to success in a real estate career, I believe that knowledge and competence trumps likeability, assuming one has to choose between the two, which of course, is not always or even usually the case. But if I had to choose a real estate agent to represent me, I'd want one who will Get the Job Done as opposed to one who will be my New Best Friend but doesn't have a clue how to manage my real estate transaction. Besides, being likeable just gets you in the door; it doesn't sell houses and doesn't lead you to a payday if you aren't competent to manage the business your likeability earns you.

I believe that if you are confident in your competence, even if you are NOT the friendliest person in the world, that confidence will be more compelling to potential clients than just being a likeable guy or gal. So you win both ways—you GET business because your demeanor inspires trust, and you GET PAID because your competence gives you a good shot at getting your transactions all the way to the closing table.

So, yes, being Really Nice gets you in the door and may win you lots of friends. And if a real estate transaction starts to sour maybe being Really Nice can even charm the client into not being too upset. But wouldn't being Really Good be a better approach? Something to shoot for?

~ ~

All rightee, so let's get back to that list of the eight attributes of an Exceptional Agent.

1. Market Mastery
2. MLS Mastery
3. Contract and Disclosure Mastery
4. Pricing Expertise
5. Photography Skills (or willingness to hire a photographer)
6. Good Problem-Solving and Negotiating
7. A Great Team
8. Great Systems in Place to Track Transactions

How important do you feel each attribute is to your own personal success? Are some far more important to you than others? Do you feel that any are irrelevant in your market or business model?

And while we're at it, how do you feel you rank on each? Some high, some not-so? Are there any that you feel are critically important to your success...yet you realize you are not as Exceptional as you could or should be?

I do hope that you agree that all, or at least most of these attributes are among what you would expect from a real estate agent you would consider hiring or referring. I would personally feel remiss if I were lacking in any of them and you know what? It would affect my confidence level in my personal promotional efforts if I didn't feel I had all these bases covered. Conversely, when you do bring all these attributes to the table...and you KNOW you bring all these attributes to the table, it gives you an air of confidence that can't be faked. It's a beautiful thing.

Chapter 3

The Eight Attributes

The next several chapters will discuss in detail what, specifically, we believe goes into being an Exceptional Agent. We've divided the various factors of Exceptional-ism into eight attributes, as described earlier:

1. Market Mastery

2. MLS Mastery

3. Contract and Disclosure Mastery

4. Pricing Expertise

5. Photography Skill

6. Problem-Solving and Negotiating Skill

7. A Great Team

8. Great Systems

Ready to get started on your journey toward being Exceptional?

Attribute #1: Market Mastery

An Exceptional Real Estate Agent understands and is "conversationally familiar" with the nuances of the local real estate market.

If I had to declare one of the eight attributes to be the one most critical to the success of a real estate agent, it would be Market Mastery, hands down. By being a Market Master, not only will you be far better at your job, but you'll also be able to easily strike up conversations with potential clients about the "real estate market" and inspire them to think of you as a knowledgeable, competent real estate professional. One they'd feel comfortable hiring or referring.

My definition of being a Market Master is that if someone tells me where they live, I get a mental image of their neighborhood, subdivision or condo building. I may not know what year their house was built or how big it is (although I might be able to guess pretty accurately), but I have a general sense of the overall ambience, the nearby amenities and can probably toss out a real estate-related anecdote or two about the area.

I call it being "conversationally familiar" with the Market when I can easily and confidently chat about the real estate in an area without resorting to the tired old "Well, I don't really know, but I'd be happy to find out for you!"

(If you'd like to read more about WHY being a Market Master is such a good idea, I discuss it in much detail in my books *Sell with Soul* and *Prospect with Soul*.)

So, How Does One Become a Market Master?

Becoming a Market Master is an ongoing process, not a one-time project. But it's a fun process, and once you start to reap the benefits of your Market Mastery efforts, you'll discover whole new dimensions to your real estate career in your confidence, your professionalism and your effectiveness in working with your clients.

> **NOTE:** Throughout this chapter (and the rest of the book for that matter), we'll refer to your "market" in a variety of contexts, and will also use the words "neighborhood," "market area," and "part of town" interchangeably.
>
> In this chapter, most references to a "market" simply mean the part of town you're in the process of mastering. If you live in a very small town, your "market" may be the entire town. If you live in a metropolitan area, the term "market" will most often refer to the particular neighborhood,

> subdivision or planned development you've decided to learn everything about.
>
> However, we'll also use the word "market" in a general sense, as in "your real estate market." In those cases, we're speaking generically as to how things are done in your area. For example, "...in some markets "previewing" active listings is allowed, even encouraged..."
>
> So, unless it's obvious we're referring to general practices in your area... Market = the Neighborhood = the Market Area = the Subdivision = the Part of Town you are committed to mastering.

Leave the GPS at Home!

As you're Mastering your Market, I'm going to challenge you to leave the GPS unit at home.

To become a true master of a market area or neighborhood, you need to be able to get TO it and THROUGH it, and understand how it fits into the Big Picture of the area, without relying on that little computer on the dashboard to guide you.

When I started selling real estate in Denver in 1996, we had no choice but to learn our way around town or risk looking like idiots when we put buyers in our cars. And that knowledge served me well, very well, throughout my career. To this day, I can draw a fairly accurate picture of the City and County of Denver, placing all neighborhoods, major cross streets, parks and shopping districts. I understand how the neighborhoods, highways, attractions and commercial districts relate to each other geographically which gave me tremendous credibility and confidence when talking with buyers about their location preferences and needs.

The funny thing is...now that I don't live in Denver and I don't sell real estate anymore, I have no clue how the Florida town I currently live in is put together. Even after living here for more than a few years, I still need the GPS to get to Walmart, the health food store and the dog park. If someone tells me they live "west of downtown" or "north of I-10," I have absolutely no mental picture of where that might be. And if I were trying to sell real estate here, that would drive me nuts.

As mentioned earlier, my definition of being a Master of Your Market is that when someone tells you where they live, you can mentally "place" their home on a map and have a reasonably accurate idea of what their neighborhood is like. If you rely on your GPS to navigate your way around town, it's likely that ability and familiarity will never fully develop.

So, as you're working toward Mastering your Market, try it the old-fashioned way. Yeah, it might be a bit frustrating and take more time, but you'll be glad you made the effort, I promise.

Identify a Market You Want to Master

Unless you work in a very small town, becoming a Master of Your Market will likely be done over the course of several months (or even years), and done one neighborhood, property type or price range at a time.

So, which market area or areas should you tackle first? Here are some ideas:

1. The market area your office serves and/or specializes in
2. The market area you live in yourself
3. A market area you'd love to live in yourself
4. A market area you've already done some business in or are currently working in with a buyer or seller
5. A market area where a lot of your friends live
6. An "up and coming" neighborhood where investors can find great deals

You can also decide to master a particular segment of your overall market that is not location-specific, such as a certain price range (for example, luxury homes or a price range in which your sphere of influence is likely to buy or sell in), or property type (for example, multi-family or vacation rental). However, for the purposes of this chapter, we'll assume that you will choose a location-related market to master.

Take a Road Trip

Once you've chosen the market you'd like to master first, let's pay it a little visit!

But before you head out, go to your MLS and print out a list of all the homes for sale in the neighborhood. If the neighborhood you've chosen is a large one and there are way too many listings to print out, that's fine, just narrow them down until you have a list of 15-20 homes.

Next, look at a map of the area and determine if the market area has any obvious "boundaries," which may include major cross-streets or other physical boundaries (such as parks or commercial districts) that form the perimeter of the area.

Next, get into your car, drive to your new favorite neighborhood (sans GPS!) and drive those boundaries to get a first-hand, face-to-face visual of how the neighborhood lays out and fits into the bigger picture of the surrounding neighborhoods. Once you've driven the perimeter, go search for the active listings you printed out, not so much to check out the listings themselves (we'll get to that!), but to help you become a better navigator of the neighborhood as you search out addresses.

This driving around may sound a bit silly, and you may get some funny looks from the residents, but remember, part of being a Market Master is being able to conjure up a mental image of an area when someone gives you a street name or address within the area you're a Master of.

Spend a Day on the MLS

Now that you've spent some time in your new favorite neighborhood, let's do a little research on what's going on there, real estate-wise. The goal of this research is to educate yourself on the facts and figures of the neighborhood, such as price ranges, square footage ranges, days on market and list-to-sales price ratios.

> **NOTE:** I use the word "ranges," not "averages." What's the difference? The typical "average" statistic is of little use to you in truly understanding your market. For example, if the *average* Days on Market (DOM) in a neighborhood is 102 days, what does that really mean? Well, it probably means that some houses sell in 2 days and some in 200, thus resulting in an *average* Days on Market statistic of 102. There may not be one house sold in the last six months that took exactly 102 days to sell! It's entirely possible, in fact, that half the houses sold in the first 30 days and the other half took six months, which would result in a DOM somewhere in the middle. Now, of course, if you look at the sold data and find that almost all the homes DID take around 102 days to sell, then, yes, that's meaningful. But part of knowing your market is knowing whether or not the *average* Days on Market is relevant or not.
>
> Same thing with the list-to-sold price. As you analyze the sold data, you'll probably see a range of list-to-sold percentages from 30% to 0% off the list price. If that's the case, do you see why it's misleading to say that "houses are selling at 92% of asking?"
>
> This is where understanding your market is far more important than memorizing it. For example, if someone asked me "how long are homes taking to sell these days?" I'd probably answer with something like, "Oh, gosh, it depends on the day and price range and the style of home, but

> overall, great houses that are priced right sell quickly—under a week sometimes even. But there is a lot of inventory and if a house isn't one of the best available, it may sit for months and months and may not even sell at all."

So, what will your research entail?

Well, if your goal is to become "conversationally familiar" with your new favorite neighborhood, I'm thinking you'd want to know the price range of the housing stock (both actives and solds), the size-range (square footage) of the inventory, the high and low Days on Market and List-to-Sold ratios.

So, fire up the MLS, run some searches and have fun with it! You might want to take notes on what you find, both to cement what you've learned into your brain so you can easily toss out some relevant statistics in casual conversation about the market *("Prices in that neighborhood range from around $150,000 to $275,000")* and to refer to in the future as the market changes *("Last year it was common for a home to be on the market several months; right now, good homes are selling in less than a week.")*, which, again, will enable you to make intelligent conversation about the market.

Neighborhood Name	High	Low
Price of Active Listings	$274,900	$149,900
Price of Sold Listings (last 6 months)	$258,750	$133,500
Square Footage of Active Listings	2,338	1,345
Days on Market of Sold Listings	368	2
List-to-Sold Price Percentage	101%	67%

Preview, Preview, Preview
(Excerpted from Chapter Six of *Prospect with Soul*)

If it's customary to preview in your market, do that. A lot. If you're not familiar with "previewing" it simply means to go look at listed houses by yourself or with another agent, not with a buyer. Some markets frown on previewing and if that's the case in yours, you might want to move. Just kidding, sort of. I advise all new agents to spend some serious quality time previewing in their first few months on the job. Like every other day if they can.

In order to be an effective previewer, you need to practice what I call "Opinionated Previewing" or "Previewing with a Purpose." When you go out to look at houses with the goal of learning your market, you should look at homes that you can compare to each other. A great example of opinionated previewing is when you preview in preparation for an open house. You're looking for other somewhat similar homes to the home you're holding open so that you can speak intelligently to visitors about the competition for this home.

Or, of course, if you're previewing for a new buyer, you'll be looking for the best homes to show him in a price range. Or, heck, maybe you just want to get a feel for what your own house is worth, so you go out and look at homes like yours. Whatever your excuse, being able to compare homes to each other helps you internalize the data you're gathering.

Here are some other ideas to Preview Opinionatedly:

- Preview all the listings built by the same builder in the neighborhood;
- Preview all the listings priced between, say, $200,000 and $250,000 (or whatever range makes sense in the market);
- Preview all the listings within three blocks of the trendy shopping district in the neighborhood;
- Preview all the homes built between 1920 and 1930 in the neighborhood;
- Preview one or two homes of each architectural "style" available in the neighborhood that are of similar square footage and price range;
- Preview all the homes with _____—fill in the blank!

Keep Up with Competing Listings

When you have a listing, you DO keep up with the listings competing with it, don't you? The ones available when you hit the market, the ones that come on the market during your listing, the ones that go under contract, expire and close? And keep your seller updated with the comings and goings of the listings in competition with theirs?

This is an excellent practice, not only in serving your seller client, but also in helping you further Master the Markets of your own listings! So, get in the habit of checking the MLS on a regular basis in the market area of all your listings, preview new listings as they come up and you know what? You may find yourself to be THE go-to guy or gal in that neighborhood because you KNOW what's what there.

Oh, and not to mention, by keeping your finger on the pulse of the market activity surrounding your listings, you'll be far more confident and, therefore, more persuasive when it comes time to make recommendations to your seller in the event your listing isn't selling.

Find Demographic Information

Okay, okay...we all know about Fair Housing laws and all the things we cannot talk about. Can't answer questions about crime...about schools...about the racial make-up of a neighborhood or where the Jewish/Muslim/Christian folk live.

But you know what? Even if we can't have those conversations with our clients, I believe it is part of being a Market Master to know the answers. (If you don't agree, you can skip this section and move onto the next).

Still with me? Okay, cool.

Let's define what we mean by "demographics." We aren't just referring to the potentially touchy subjects of race and religion, but also age, gender, income, family status and home ownership.

The lowest-tech way to get a feel for the demographics of a neighborhood is to simply drive around (or walk around) and see who you see. Maybe you'll see a lot of young couples without children, or conversely, a lot of retired-looking folks. Maybe you'll see a lot of expensive sedans or conversely, four-wheel drive trucks. Maybe you'll see a large church, synagogue, temple or other place of worship that clearly has a strong local membership. Maybe you'll notice a large homosexual population or shops that cater to families with children.

You may also be able to get specific demographic information online, although the relevance of that information will depend heavily on how your city collects, tracks and categorizes such information. Just search for <your neighborhood name> demographics and see how you do.

What about Crime Statistics?

As a Master of my Market, I want to understand how that market area compares to others with regards to crime rates. Again, I probably can't share that information with my clients, but I want to know it...just because...I want to know it.

If you'd also like to become familiar with the crime rates in the Market you're Mastering (or heck, city-wide), just google <your city> crime statistics and see what you find. Once you find a good website for crime statistics, you may certainly share the link with your clients upon request!

If you'd like to see how I addressed the Demographics question with my clients, you can visit my old website: www.CharmingOldDenver.com and click on "Denver Demographics."

Read Other Agents' Blogs and Newsletters

Why not? We're not advising you to steal anyone's content or otherwise mis-use it—just learn from it. It's there...out in the open and there's nothing in the world wrong with checking out what your competition is doing and learning a little something about the market in the process!

Identify Alternatives to the Market You're Mastering

One of the most powerful ways to become a Master of Your Market is to know what the alternatives are to the Market you've Mastered. By "alternatives," I mean neighborhoods that offer similar features and amenities, but might offer lower prices, better highway access, higher-rated schools or any other combination of features and amenities that a buyer who is interested in the Market you're Mastering might want to explore.

Most buyers won't be fixated on one particular neighborhood; they'll be willing to consider alternatives if they aren't finding exactly what they want in one. So, the more conversationally familiar you are with the alternatives, the more credibility you'll have with your buyers.

Identifying viable alternatives to a neighborhood is an ongoing process; one that you'll develop a keener sense for the more familiar you become with the Markets you Master. But to get the process started, ask YOURSELF what neighborhoods you might consider if you were interested in purchasing a home in the Market you're Mastering, but couldn't afford it or needed to be closer to downtown or wanted a better school district or whatever.

For example, if the Market you're in the process of Mastering offers newer 3 bedroom/2.5 bath homes on large lots priced from $200,000 to $300,000, which neighborhoods in the same general part of town also offer newer homes with family-friendly floor plans with reasonably sized lots for $150,000 to $200,000?

Or if the Market you're Mastering offers charming older homes and is in a trendy (read, expensive) part of town, are there other older neighborhoods with similar charm that aren't quite as trendy (yet)?

Just give it some thought. If you were shopping for a home in the Market you're Mastering, what other neighborhoods would you consider also? Perhaps those neighborhoods will be the next Markets you choose to Master!

Other Master-Your-Market Activities

✓ Identify the schools that serve the market area

If you live in a metropolitan area, the information is likely readily available online. Just search for <your city> Public Schools, enter the zip code or codes of your neighborhood and away you go. Once you have the names of the individual schools (grade schools, junior high and senior high schools), you can probably Google each name to get more detailed information about each, such as ratings, rankings, demographics and enrollment, although as we discussed earlier, Fair Housing laws will limit what you can actually DO with this information.

If you can't find anything online about the school system, the information may be available on your MLS, or you can contact the Board of Education and ask for guidance.

Next time you're out and about, drive by each school so that you recognize it by sight and location. You'll be glad you did when you're out with buyers and they ask you about that big brick building on the corner!

✓ Patronize the businesses in the Market you're Mastering

Hey, you gotta shop somewhere…you gotta eat sometime…you gotta get your hair cut, your dog groomed and your dry-cleaning done, so why not do it in The Market You're Mastering? Not only will you be likely to meet people who have real estate needs in the area, but you'll also be able to speak intelligently to clients about the local businesses and amenities.

✓ Identify all landmark buildings in The Market you're Mastering

Drive around The Market you're Mastering and make notes of the buildings you see that aren't readily identifiable. Schools, churches, rest homes, etc. Find out what they are so when you're working with a buyer and the buyer asks, "What's that?" you'll know the answer!

JENNIFER'S BLOG: A Big SOI A-HA Moment!

For years now I've been extolling the virtues of a Sphere of Influence (SOI) business model—that is, basing your business on the power of your personal relationships instead of the power of your marketing budget. I've claimed that I ran a nearly 100% SOI business literally from Day One—a business that was successful by anyone's definition—in which virtually all of my business came directly or indirectly from the people I knew. I've implied (or outright said) that I never pursued business from strangers.

I've been lying to y'all. Didn't mean to, but I have. Sorry about that.

Here's the thing. A lot of my business DID come from my SOI, no question about that. I was lucky to have a large circle of acquaintances when I entered the business and was able to generate quite a bit of support among the people who knew me. God bless 'em.

However, a not-insignificant amount of my business through the years DID come from total strangers. People I had no personal relationship with, nor did we know anyone in common. While I've always referred to these sales as SOI-generated, technically, they really weren't. THESE PEOPLE WERE STRANGERS TO ME.

But I'll stand behind my statement (modified slightly) that I never actively pursued business from strangers.

I never cold-called, I never door-knocked, I rarely advertised. I never called a FSBO. I didn't farm.

Yes, I GOT business from strangers, but that business was never the result of PURSUING it.

So, um, Jennifer... care to enlighten us as to how you GOT business from strangers if you didn't PURSUE business from strangers?

Happy to.

They say that Luck is When Opportunity Meets Preparation. BINGO!

Opportunity: Being out in the world with a smile on your face and your antenna up.

Preparation: Being ready to speak intelligently and knowledgeably about the local real estate market.

Don't want to prospect? Then don't. Spend that time learning the heck out of your market. Preview, preview, preview. Read neighborhood newspapers. Preview some more. Visit neighborhood grocery stores and shopping districts. Preview. Visit new home communities, attend meetings on Transit Oriented Development. Preview. Know your office inventory inside and out.

When a Stranger Calls...(on one of your listings or while you're on floor duty), you'll get 'em. When an open house visitor expresses an interest in the neighborhood...you'll get 'em. When another guest at a wedding wants to talk real estate investment...you'll get 'em.

KNOWING YOUR MARKET is the best way to "prospect" to strangers. No fancy business card, well-rehearsed elevator speech or slick closing technique will beat the confidence that exudes from you when you know your stuff. It's magnetic

~ ~

Attribute #2: MLS Mastery

An Exceptional Real Estate Agent is an expert in the local Multiple Listing Service.

Next on our list of the Eight Attributes of an Exceptional Agent is MLS Mastery. Yawn? Perhaps (although if you're yawning about THIS attribute, just wait till our next attribute, Contract and Disclosure Mastery.)

Nah, seriously, MLS Mastery may not be the sexiest topic on the planet, and truthfully, if you've been practicing real estate for a while, you may already be a Master—but let's just make sure…for sure, deal?

What is an MLS Master?

An MLS Master…

1. Is not intimidated by his MLS; he knows his way around the system and while he may not use all of the bells and whistles offered, he is an expert on the features he does use.

2. Has complete confidence in his ability to find the data he seeks—all of it—even if some of the data he needs has been input incorrectly by others.

3. Is able to take the data provided by the MLS and create coherent reports, proposals or packages that are easily understandable by his clients.

Why Be an MLS Master?

At the time of this writing, the MLS is still the primary database of information real estate agents need to practice their craft. If you are not proficient in the use of your market's MLS, your clients will suffer for it, and therefore, so will you. If, when you are searching for that needle-in-a-haystack home for your fussy buyers…or when you are preparing a market analysis for your new seller clients…or trying to interpret the recent market activity surrounding your non-selling listing—if you do not have a Masterful command of the MLS and the data it makes available, the results of your efforts will be incomplete…or perhaps even dead wrong.

Ack! Let's not let that happen to you…or your clients.

How to Achieve MLS Mastery

Easy enough. Education...and practice.

First, seriously consider taking a class on your MLS. Even if you consider yourself a Master already, I'll bet $10 you'll learn something in class that will change the way you use the MLS, especially if your local MLS has been upgraded lately. I dread sitting in class more than anyone (especially a class full of techno-phobic real estate agents), but I'm pretty sure the half-day invested will be time well spent.

Then...practice, practice, practice.

Find YOUR Dream Home

So, what sort of home (available in your market) would qualify as your "dream home?" Make a list of the features it would offer, including your ideal location, vintage (i.e., age of the home), preferred school district, number of bedrooms, baths and parking spaces, any special features such as a swimming pool, a bonus room/man cave, a separate guest house, finished basement, zoning for horses, mountain view, whatever!

Then, get on the MLS and go FIND your dream home.

If you have fun with this, do it some more with friends—ask THEM to describe their dream home for you and go find it.

Search Your Own Neighborhood

If you live in a residential area, how about combining your MLS Mastery efforts with getting to know more about your own neighborhood, from a real estate perspective?

Identify the lowest priced and highest priced homes in your neighborhood. The smallest and the largest properties. The lowest and highest Days on Market among the solds of the last three months, six months, twelve months. How many homes have swimming pools, central air conditioning, 3+ car garages? Have any homes sold in less than a week in the last six months? Are there homes that have been on the market over a year?

Your MLS, Line by Line

Do you know what each and every field on your full MLS printout relates to? Even the ones that agents typically leave blank? Do you know where the information comes from that is used to complete the fields when new listings are input?

Print out a "full" listing (that is—the version of an MLS listing entry that includes every single field) and go through it field by field to identify any that you aren't quite sure either what they refer to or where the information came from (for example, school district information or zoning code). Commit to spending at least an hour going through it—as you run into fields you aren't quite sure of—go GET sure of them, either by asking the office manager (or whoever is primarily responsible for entering new listings), another agent, or probably best, the website of your MLS provider; hopefully they provide detailed explanations of all the fields.

Again, this doesn't sound like the most fun way to spend an hour, but I'll bet you'll learn something that will make you glad you invested the time...something that puts you closer to being an Exceptional Real Estate Agent.

Mastering Your MLS Reports

Another area of your MLS you'll want to master is the reporting section.

Let's define what we mean by "reports." Reports are typically printable (and perhaps emailable or linkable) summaries of information. The information contained in each individual report may or may not be customizable. A report can be as simple as a list of addresses with the basic specs (# bedrooms, baths, sqft) or as detailed as a full-detail page for each address, including broker comments.

How might you use the reporting function of your MLS?

Lots of ways!

Here are some ideas:

1. Create your own custom CMAs[2] (Comparative Market Analyses) to use during listing appointments.

2. Create Market Update reports for your current seller clients.

---

[2]While there is CMA-specific software available, you may find that, once you master the MLS reporting feature, you'll prefer to create your own. Why might you prefer this? Because creating custom reports forces you to more closely analyze the data instead of simply relying on the system to do it for you. This helps you in two ways—first, your CMA will likely be more accurate if you create it yourself, and second, you'll be much more familiar with the data as you're explaining it to a potential seller. Besides, many CMA programs include a lot of fluff and meaningless information that looks impressive but doesn't accomplish the goal of helping the seller (and you!) understand what's really going on in the marketplace.

3. Provide both summarized and detailed spec sheets to buyers to refer to as you show them homes.

4. Create comparative reports for buyers to help them determine the market value of a home they're interested in.

5. Create comparative reports for yourself to help you figure out why a listing isn't selling.

6. Create market reports to use in your blog, on your website or in other marketing.

7. Create informational packages to make available at open houses.

8. Create and offer basic market analyses to your sphere of influence.

So, if you haven't already, fire up your MLS and find the reporting section.

Choose a few of the ideas above and, using the reporting feature of your MLS, create sample reports you'll be proud to use with your prospects and clients in the (near) future.

Read the Rules and Regulations of Your MLS
Having trouble sleeping? This next project might help.

Dig up the Rules and Regulations of your MLS. In the olden days, they were found in the Big Book of Listings; today they are probably available online at your Board or MLS's website, or perhaps in all that paperwork you signed when registering for access to the MLS.

No, it probably won't be the most exciting reading, but then again, you might be surprised. MLS boards can be a bit persnickety about how the information from their database is used, so there may well be some information in there that will keep you out of trouble down the road.

Attribute #3: Contract and Disclosure Mastery

Exceptional Real Estate Agents understand and can explain each and every provision in the contracts and disclosures they present.

If you ask most real estate agents, regardless of their level of experience, if they are 100% comfortable with their Mastery of the contracts and disclosures they use in their real estate practice, chances are the majority of them will confess (if only to themselves) that they are not. In fact, I'll go first...*I, Jennifer Allan-Hagedorn have some "soft-spots" in my Mastery of the State of Colorado's real estate contracts and disclosures and I will admit to bluffing my way through certain provisions that I never really quite "got."*

How about you?

Interestingly, brand new agents fresh out of real estate school—who have yet to set a showing, open a lockbox or even log onto their MLS, may have the most up-to-date technical knowledge of the provisions found in their state's contracts and disclosures, although they are likely sorely lacking in a real-world understanding of them. Conversely, those of us with years of experience probably understand the big picture that is made up of all those individual provisions, but may not recall exactly what each individual provision is intended to convey or negotiate.

Regardless of where you fall in the years-of-experience spectrum, it's a good idea to review your contracts and disclosures from time to time, and that's what this chapter will do for you. Reading this chapter may not be the most fun hour or two or three you'll ever spend, but if you do the exercises we suggest, you'll come out on the other side a far more knowledgeable real estate practitioner—and therefore an Exceptional one. And being Exceptional is what it's all about, right?

The Process

On the following pages, we will describe a systematic process for Mastering Your Contracts and Disclosures, both for buyer clients and seller clients. The process consists of these steps:

- ✓ Review the contract line by line and highlight provisions you don't fully understand.
- ✓ Research the meaning/implication of each provision you highlighted.

- ✓ Identify the required disclosures for each type of client (buyer and seller).
- ✓ Review each disclosure line by line and highlight provisions you don't fully understand.
- ✓ Research the meaning/implication of each provision you highlighted.
- ✓ Role-play, explaining the entire contract and disclosure package to a buyer or seller.

Sound fun? Eh, maybe not, but let's get to it anyway.

Your Buyer Contracts and Disclosures

Step One: Pull out (or print out) a blank copy of the Buyer Purchase Agreement used in your area. Go through it line by line, reading each provision out loud or even role-play explaining it to a buyer. Every time you encounter a provision you don't fully understand, highlight it to return to later.

Step Two: You know what comes next. Research each and every provision that you highlighted. Here are some resources that might help:

1. The Real Estate Manual put out by your Board or Real Estate Commission

2. Your broker, trainer or a more experienced agent

3. Your local Board or Real Estate Commission's websites

4. Your best friend Google

Step Three: Identify the disclosures that are required to be completed and submitted with a purchase agreement. Your office manager likely has a list of these for you. Depending on your office policy and state law, these disclosures might include Lead-Based Paint Disclosure, a Mold Disclosure, a RESPA Disclosure (if your company offers other real estate-related services), an Agency Disclosure and a Seller's Property Disclosure.

Gather up blank copies of each, and...

Step Four: Go through every line on every disclosure document and highlight any provisions you don't fully understand, then...

Step Five: Research every highlighted provision so that you understand the meaning and implications of each, and can confidently explain them to a buyer client.

Step Six: Role-play the entire process from start to finish with a mock buyer. Draft up the contract, prepare the disclosures, explain each and every provision to your "buyer," obtain initials and signatures everywhere required, put the package together and pretend to make the appropriate number of copies.

Now, wasn't that fun?

A Word (or two) About Buyer Agency

While this chapter isn't about the pros and cons of buyer agency (To take or not to take? To require or not to require?), it's worth mentioning that if you do intend to offer/take/require buyer agency, you need to understand and be able to fully explain each and every provision contained in your state's buyer agency contract.

If you'd like to read more about my opinion of Buyer Agency, refer to Chapter Eight in *Sell with Soul*. (Okay, here's a sneak peak. I think it's obnoxious to require Buyer Agency upfront—I wouldn't dream of signing a Buyer Agency Agreement at my first meeting with an agent, so I wouldn't dream of asking my potential clients to sign one either!)

INTERLUDE: Dates & Deadlines

Every real estate Purchase Agreement has dates and deadlines that need to be negotiated. It's your job as the buyer representative to understand what each date and deadline refers to so that you can draft an offer that both protects your buyer client—and will also be perceived as reasonable by the seller.

Therefore, you need to have a Big Picture understanding of the flow of a real estate transaction so you know how much time to allot for each date and deadline you'll propose (or negotiate in a counter-offer). If you have this understanding, filling in the date and deadline fields in your offer will be mostly common sense, assuming, of course, that you also understand what each date or deadline refers to!

When completing the dates and deadlines section of a Purchase Agreement, always have a calendar open in front of you; it will make a world of difference. You'll see where the weekends and holidays fall, you'll have a better visual of how much time you're giving your buyer to perform — and there's just something about seeing how the dates you're filling in relate to the days of the week and month.

If you don't have a lot of experience working with buyers and completing Purchase Agreements, I highly recommend that you sit in with other agents who are going through a Purchase Agreement with their buyer clients. As many times as you can. With as many different agents as you can. You'll find that every agent handles the dates and deadlines section a little differently and since there is no One Right Way to do it, the more exposure you get to various approaches, the better.

Once you get the hang of it, filling out the dates and deadlines section of a Purchase Agreement is pretty easy. And every time you go through a transaction with a buyer client, you'll fine-tune your own approach to negotiating dates and deadlines.

Now, on to Your Seller Documents

So, you are now a Master of the Buyer Purchase Agreement and Disclosures!

Of course, that means it's now time to start Mastering Your Listing Contracts and Disclosures.

And as you can probably guess, the process to do this will look familiar to you.

But first, a few comments about how Listing Agreements and Disclosures are different from Buyer Purchase Agreement and Disclosures (besides the obvious!).

While most buyer contracts and disclosures today are completed on a computer in your office, listing agreements are still often completed sitting at the seller's dining room table. Therefore, it's perfectly acceptable to hand-write[3] much of the paperwork, but be aware that you may not have the "buffer" of your computer screen to hide behind or be able to prepare ahead of time! In other words, you'll need to be able to complete the listing agreement while someone is sitting across the table watching your every move and likely making conversation with you as you do it.

Fortunately, listing agreements are typically shorter than Purchase Agreements and often much less detailed. And since it's an agreement between you and your client, there isn't an adversarial third party involved who will be negotiating the terms of your agreement once you've drafted it up. Once you and your seller client have reached agreement on the terms of the listing, you won't be presenting it to someone else for further negotiation.

So...

Step One: Pull out (or print out) a blank copy of the Listing Agreement used in your area. Go through it line by line, reading each provision out loud or even role-play explaining it to a seller. Every time you encounter a provision you don't fully understand, highlight it to return to later.

> [3]It's a good practice to prepare as much of the listing agreement ahead of time as you can on your contract software, filling in the blanks that won't be up for discussion when you meet with your seller. Fields to be pre-completed might include the property address and legal description and the names of the owners. Some agents fill in their listing fee(s) so as not to give the impression that their fee(s) is/are negotiable. Fields that probably should not be pre-completed (unless you've discussed them ahead of time) include the price, the inclusions and exclusions and the listing start date and expiration date.

Step Two: You know what comes next. Research each and every provision that you highlighted. Here are some resources that might help:

1. The Real Estate Manual put out by your Board or Real Estate Commission

2. Your broker, trainer or a more experienced agent

3. Your local Board or Real Estate Commission's websites

4. Your best friend Google

Step Three: Identify the disclosures that are required to be completed by a seller. Your office manager likely has a list of these for you—depending on your office policy and state law, these disclosures may include Lead-Based Paint Disclosure, a Mold Disclosure, a RESPA Disclosure (if your company offers other real estate-related services), an Agency Disclosure and a Seller's Property Disclosure.

Gather up blank copies of each, and...

Step Four: Go through every line on every disclosure document and highlight any provisions you don't fully understand, then...

Step Five: Research every highlighted provision so that you understand the meaning and implications of each, and can confidently explain them to a seller client.

Step Six: Role-play the entire process from start to finish with a mock seller. Draft up the contract, prepare the disclosures, explain each and every provision to your "seller," obtain initials and signatures everywhere required, put the package together to turn in to your office manager.

> **NOTE:** In the real world, should you return to your office and recreate the listing agreement on your contract software now that you have all the fields completed? You can, but it's probably not necessary. Doing so will require you to meet again with the seller, go through the agreement again with them to ensure that you got everything right and have them re-sign. There are probably better uses of your time and energy.

Attribute #4: Pricing Expertise

Exceptional Real Estate Agents understand how location, condition, features and amenities (or lack thereof) affect the value of the properties in their market area.

When I was an active real estate agent, I took the pricing of a home very seriously—whether I was interviewing for a listing, trying to figure out why a listing wasn't selling or working with a buyer who wanted to make an offer. It just seemed like the obvious thing to do—to spend a lot of time researching the information available, both online and what was out there in the market. And then, it also seemed obvious to me that I should present the findings from my research in a clear, coherent and persuasive manner to my client.

And I did...I'd spend hours doing market analyses for sellers, and when working with buyers, I'd do detailed evaluations of what I thought the market value of the property they were considering was—especially when working with investors who not only needed to know the current value, but also and even more importantly, the potential future value after renovation.

Because I chose to work from home almost from Day One, as a newbie I wasn't up to speed on what other agents did to prepare for their listing appointments from a pricing perspective, or what they did to help their buyers come up with an appropriate offer price. So it came as quite a surprise to me a few years into my career when I decided to hang out more at my real estate office to discover that most of the agents in that office did very little in-depth research—they just printed off a bunch of comparables and headed out the door with their pile!

To be honest, I wondered if there was something wrong with ME that I simply wasn't that "good" at pricing homes that I couldn't just print out a bunch of nearby listings, take a cursory look at my printouts and come up with The Right Price. Or that when I tried to use the fancy Comparative Market Analysis (CMA) programs, I never felt good about the price the program spit out, much less my comfort explaining the results to my client. What was wrong with ME that I felt the need to do much more research and, frankly, much more WORK to come up with a price I felt comfortable presenting to my client?

Well, in retrospect...and with the confidence that experience and maturity brings, I now realize that of course it's better to do MORE research and MORE preparation than to do LESS research and LESS preparation! Moreover, there was nothing in the world wrong with me because I felt compelled to invest some time and energy into properly pricing my listings and properly advising my buyers.

So, in this chapter, I'm going to share with you the process I believe is the right way to properly price property and, you know what? It is a lot of work, although the better you know your market, and the more practice you have putting it all together, the easier it will be for you. My first CMA took me three solid days to put together; later in my career I could do one in an hour or so (not counting the time I spent previewing).

I'll get to that process here in a bit, but first I want to talk about why I consider proper pricing to be an art, even more so than a science.

The "Art" of Pricing

By "art" I mean that properly pricing a home is not simply a matter of ciphering the facts, figures, statistics and formulas. Yes, objective parameters ("science") will certainly factor in to the right price, but there's more to it than that.

We've all seen the phenomena of a house that looks great on paper, only to discover when we show it that it's not so great, even if the MLS specifications and description are more or less accurate. Or two houses that look exactly the same on paper and even from the outside, but once you go in, have completely different appeal from each other. I remember so many times when I'd start working with a new buyer, I'd pull up a bunch of listings that seemed to fit his or her requirements and then after previewing, reject all but a few of them, even though their specifications and descriptions sounded great "on paper."

There are also other factors that affect the Right Price for a home that have little to do with the home itself. For example, a home that is hard to show may be worth less on the open market even if it's exactly the same as the other homes in the area that aren't hard to show. If a home has unusual possession requirements—let's say that it's tenant-occupied and so the new owner can't take possession of the home for three months after closing—that will affect market value. If the seller insists on being home during showings or in leaving his barking dogs locked in the laundry room or back yard, thus limiting a buyer's access to the home—that can very well affect market value.

The thing is—when you put any road blocks in the way of a buyer falling in love with a home with showing restrictions or other limitations, you reduce the number of buyers who will consider purchasing the home and when you reduce the number of buyers who might buy the home, the market value will likely be adversely affected. So, if you do run into a situation where the homeowner insists on making the home difficult to fall in love with, you will almost certainly need to price the home to be attractive enough for buyers and their agents to put up with the inconvenience and look at it anyway.

Of course, while this isn't the subject of this chapter, the best solution is to persuade the seller not to do anything that reduces the subjective appeal of the home, but for our purposes right now, just know that the seller's level of cooperation in the marketing process IS a factor in determining market value.

> **NOTE:** This chapter is not about listing appointment strategy, but rather about properly pricing homes, although the two are, of course, interrelated. If you'd like to read more about the SWS-approach to listing appointments, refer to my book *The More Fun You Have Selling Real Estate, the More Real Estate You Will Sell*; there are several chapters devoted to the subject.

INTERLUDE: Pricing by Price Per Square Foot (PSF)—PUH-LEAZE NO!

Let me take a break and rant about the concept of pricing by price per square foot. Don't do it. Just don't do it. I don't care if everyone in your office uses that approach, except in very specific situations, it's wrong. It's lazy, it's unprofessional and it's just wrong.

It's wrong.

Unfortunately, many home sellers and real estate agents believe in pricing by PSF and it's hard to talk them out of it. PSF pricing is 'easy' to understand and difficult to explain why it's wrong if someone is bound and determined to believe it is right.

But let's give it a shot.

First, let's define Price Per Square Foot

A 2,000 square foot home priced at $250,000 has a PSF of $125 ($250,000/2,000=$125).

A 2,500 square foot home priced at $250,000 has a PSF of $100 ($250,000/2,500=$100).

The PSF of a home is the Price divided by the Square Footage.

Let's say that you are preparing a market analysis for a house that is 1,850 square feet.

While reviewing the recent sales, you see that other homes in the area are selling at an **average** of $133 per square foot, with a range of $100—$150. So, if we assume that your potential listing is "average" then, using the price per square foot approach, you would declare it to be worth $246,050.

$$1{,}850 \times \$133 = \$246{,}050$$

But what if it's a little better than average? If you adjust the psf by only $10 (e.g., $143 psf), you now have a market value of $264,550—nearly $20,000 more! What, exactly, are you basing that $10 figure on, and is $10 the right figure? If you're off by just a few dollars, it affects your suggested market value by thousands.

50 | The Exceptional Real Estate Agent

Or what if the "average" home in the area has 2.5 bathrooms, but yours has 3.5? What if your potential listing has a three-car garage while the "average" home has just two garage spaces? What if your potential listing has a custom gourmet kitchen, but the others have the original builder-grade kitchens?

Or conversely, what if your potential listing reeks of smoke or cat urine?

The thing is, the price per square foot of a home is simply a piece of data, not a pricing tool. If you look at a professional appraisal, you'll see that on all those pages, there is only one line item (maybe two) that even mentions price per square foot. The bulk of the appraisal consists of valuing the specific features the subject home includes compared to the features included or not included in nearby comparable properties, NOT the price per square foot of the subject and comparables.

But besides the fact that pricing by square foot is inaccurate, it's also unprofessional and won't do anything to increase a seller's confidence in you as a competent professional. I mean, seriously—anyone with access to MLS data and a calculator can figure out what the average PSF is for a list of properties; do we really want to imply that the extent of our professional pricing expertise is limited to some fourth grade math equations?

A few years ago I talked with an agent about selling a home of mine that was in a unique area, on acreage and had a lot of custom features. So, how did she suggest I price it? Well, she just said that homes on acreage in the area were selling at an average of $100 psf, so the approximate market value of my house was $235,000.

<JAH shakes head.>

Now wait a cotton-pickin' minute...first, I'm pretty sure MY acreage wasn't exactly the same as the other homes' acreage, I'm guessing that my kitchen and baths were nicer than (or worse than) the other homes on acreage, and that the lack of a garage on my property versus the other homes that had garages might also factor in? And why should my home be priced according to the "average" psf in the area? What if it's a little nicer or not quite as nice? And again, if you do the math, the difference of just $10 a foot in the psf—say, $100 versus $110 makes a big difference in the price.

When should you use PSF to price a home?

The price per square foot data can be a reasonably good indicator of value when you are comparing identical condos or newer homes by the same builder in a tract home subdivision. But you should never use PSF as your only method of pricing any residential property.

Anyway, that's a soapbox I love talking about and I get very irritated when anyone tries to sell me on the concept of pricing per square foot, so thank you for indulging my tirade. And if you ever interview to list one of my houses, you better not come at me with any price per square foot nonsense ☺.

Your Listing Appointment

So, let's set the stage. You have a listing appointment scheduled with a homeowner in, say, four days, so you have four days to get ready for your appointment.

What I'm going to share with you is how I handled the pricing part of listing appointments and, therefore, the way I think it ought to be done—or at least, what makes the most sense to me. Of course, your business is your business, so feel free to take what you like from my approach and reject anything that doesn't suit you or your market. But remember, we're shooting for Exceptional.

The Two-Step Approach

I believe in a minimum of a two-step listing process—and not because I feel it's a better "sales" strategy but rather because I feel doing it that way contributes toward coming up with a more accurate price.

What I mean by a two-step process is that the goal of my first meeting with a seller was NOT to *present* information, but rather to *gather* information so that I could come up with an accurate price. It always bewildered me that an agent could claim to be able to properly price a home for sale before he's even seen it—sure he might have a general idea of the price ranges for the area, but, at least in my Denver market, seeing the interior of the home made a world of difference in the price I'd eventually recommend.

Using that approach—that you're going to spend your time with the seller at your first meeting *gathering* information, not *presenting* information—there isn't a lot you need to do from a pricing perspective to prepare for the meeting!

Okay, so you meet with the seller and spend your time gathering information. You look at the house and take notes on special features and potential obstacles to sale. You do your best to find out what the sellers are willing and able to do or not do to maximize the marketability of the home to help you get it sold for them. There are other things you'll talk about, of course, but as far as pricing is concerned, these are the two factors you want to know as much about as you can—the house itself and the seller's willingness to be cooperative.

So, you finish up your appointment, promise to be in touch, and head back to the office to put your CMA together.

Creating Your CMA

In creating a CMA, following is the order in which I approached the process, but there's nothing magic about it—feel free to do the following steps in any order that suits you.

Preview the Competition

The first thing I would do was to preview all the current competition—and by that I mean visit all the homes currently listed that a buyer interested in my potential listing would also look at.

When previewing the competition, preview as many as you can—one or two or three won't do the trick, shoot for at least six or seven. Which homes should you preview? Well, again, as many as you can. With every house you tour, you gain a little better grasp on the up-to-the-minute marketplace which makes it much easier to pinpoint the proper price range to recommend. It just happens naturally. As you look at the competition, you'll start to get a feel for where your potential listing falls in the scheme of things, and the more competing homes you look at, the more confident you'll be in that feeling.

Preview all comparable houses priced within 10-15% on each side of where you think the price of your listing will fall. So for example, if you are thinking the home is worth somewhere around $300,000, you would preview everything priced between $250,000 and $350,000.

Always preview the low outliers. A "low outlier" is a house that looks good (and comparable) on paper, but seems to be a screaming deal. You need to know why it's priced so well…but hasn't sold. There probably is a good reason. If there isn't, then this is the listing to beat.

How about the high outliers? The houses that are priced way above the rest, which are probably getting your seller all excited? Look at those, too. Chances are that they're just grossly overpriced (and the more houses you look at, the more certain you'll be of this). Or, there might be something really fabulous about them and you need to know what it is.

As you're setting your previews, note if any homes are difficult to show. That will definitely affect market value.

As you're previewing the active listings, realize that the houses you're previewing are two things: 1) the competition for your upcoming listing and 2) houses that haven't sold. Some agents don't preview because they don't think the active listings are relevant. "All that matters is SOLD." I disagree. What's

SOLD is not competing with your upcoming listing and knowing what buyers will be comparing to your listing is critical.

You also need to know why that active competition hasn't sold. Especially if it appears to be "priced well." You'll never know for sure why a house hasn't sold by looking at the MLS, although you may have your suspicions. But it's not as if the listing agent is going to mention the strong cat urine smell in the MLS or point out that there's no bathroom on the main floor.

So, as you're previewing, ask yourself...

WHY hasn't this house sold?

WHAT makes it superior (or inferior) to my listing?

HOW could the listing agent do a better job marketing this home?

WHO is the ideal buyer for this property and is it the same ideal buyer that mine will attract?

Training yourself to ask these questions at every house you preview makes you a better previewer-of-property, and therefore, a better pricer-of-property. It also helps you to remember each house so you can speak intelligently about the competition with your seller when discussing pricing, as well as down the road when that home's status changes (sells, withdraws or reduces the price), you'll be able to nod and say to yourself, "Hmmmm, I thought so!"

By the way, if "previewing" is not allowed in your market, do this instead...bring printouts of the listings you would consider to be competition with you—drive by all the homes and note which ones appear to be the most comparable to your potential listing. Note anything you can see from the exterior that would affect market value positively or negatively and, when you get home, look through the photos of all the listings and do your best. Honestly, I feel very lucky to have worked in a market where previewing wasn't just allowed—it was encouraged and if that's the case in your market, take advantage of it since that's not the case everywhere.

So, that's previewing the active competition.

Research the Solds

After you've previewed the competition, the next step is to evaluate the SOLD data from the MLS.

Unfortunately, evaluating SOLD data is an imperfect process. The problem with using SOLDs in your market analysis is, unless you've been a previewing mad(wo)man over the last eight months, you probably haven't seen the inside of the properties, and now it's too late. So you have to rely on the MLS description—a very risky proposition!

But we'll do our best.

Print off all the SOLDs that seem to be comparable, even if they're much higher or lower than your assumption of the market value of your listing. Drive by all of them! Pay special attention to the outliers—the ones that seem to have sold way out of whack to the rest of the market, or whose Days on Market (DOM) statistic is unusually low or high.

There's a good chance your drive-by will reveal the reason for the out-of-line price or DOM. Perhaps there's a commercial building next door, behind or across the street. Or the home sits on a corner lot that doesn't have a private back yard, or any back yard at all. Maybe it's a pop-top done wrong and doesn't fit in with the neighborhood. Or a busy street with a bus stop in the front yard.

Or conversely, you might see that it has a stellar location with an extra-large lot, a mountain view, or around the corner from a popular coffee shop which explains the quick sale or high price.

If the reason for the outlying price and/or DOM isn't obvious from your drive-by, go line-by line through the MLS listing. Is it missing a garage in a market that expects garages? No basement? One bathroom? Obviously, if the interior photos show that it needs work, that's relevant. Check the private broker comments to see if there were any obvious limitations on access.

If all else fails and you really feel a particular house is a good comparable, but the sales price isn't making sense, call the listing agent. Hopefully they'll be helpful in helping you understand why the house sold at the price it did. Or, maybe not. But give it a try.

It really is the outliers that give you the most grief when looking at the SOLDs. There probably are some sold listings that fall right in line with what you're thinking the price of your listing ought to be, but the ones that don't can give you fits. The more research you do on these outliers will not only make your CMA stronger, but will give you an air of confidence when going through your CMA with a seller.

While you're looking at the sold data, you should also include a review of the pending sales—while you may not be able to find out what the sales prices of the pendings are, they should definitely be included in your CMA. If the home is vacant, you might be able to preview these listings while you're out previewing the actives, which will give you even more knowledge about what's actually happening in that market TODAY.

Putting it All Together

Okay... so what do we have now?

We have a list of active comparable listings which I call the Active Competition, a list of the pending sales, which I call Pending Sales, and a list of comparable sales, which I call the Recent Comparable Sales.

There are two things we need to do with all this information...first—USE it to price the home and second—put it all together in a coherent analysis to present to the seller.

So, let's talk for a minute about that—about putting it all together in a coherent analysis, aka CMA. HOW do you put it all together?

CMA Software?

Well, many agents use CMA software—that is, software that was created to actually do CMAs for you—all you do is plug in the property address and voilà! You have a beautiful 32-page CMA complete with graphs and charts and numbers and such.

Personally, I'm not a fan of CMA software. Now, I must confess that I'm a bit of a control freak when it comes to my work—I don't really trust anyone else to do it right, and that includes pricing a home for sale. Because, remember...pricing a home properly is both ART and SCIENCE and there's no way a program can factor in the Art of it and, frankly, I don't think they get the Science of it all that right either.

The other reason I don't like CMA software is because I feel I need to be intimately familiar with the data that goes into my pricing recommendation—and that the research I do to properly price a home gives me the confidence that the price I come up with is correct, and when I have that confidence, I'm much more persuasive with a reluctant seller than if I simply shoved a fancy report under his nose without being able to conversationally discuss the pieces and parts of it.

At one point in my career, I decided to try the CMA software approach and took it one step further—I had my assistant do my CMA's for me—and OMGoodness...the first time I met with a seller, fancy schmantzy CMA that I'd had very little input in creating in hand, I felt like an idiot. I tried it a few more times and the same thing happened, so I abandoned that strategy pretty quickly.

That said, I did utilize an appraisal-type CMA program behind the scenes—I'd plug in all the data, let it do the number crunching and see what market value it spit out, and I did use it as a guide in my pricing. But I selected the comparables and made manual adjustments to them as I saw fit—for example, if one comparable had a better or worse location than my subject property, I'd adjust for that, or if one had hardwood floors and the other didn't, I'd manually adjust for that since that was a big deal in the Denver market I worked in.

Anyway, you're probably asking how I prepared my CMA's if I didn't use CMA software...well, I just used the reporting feature of my MLS (see Attribute #2). I created the reports I felt were useful, customized them, and put it all together myself.

My point is that I believe the more your fingerprints are all over your market analysis, the more accurate it will be and the more persuasive YOU will be when presenting it to a seller.

Okay, so back to our data.

Price That Property!

If you've truly done your research as I've described so far, you will find in most cases that the right price—or at least the right price range is becoming obvious.

But remember...again...pricing is both art and science. So before you smack a price on the listing, let's take a step back and ask your gut how it feels about the figure your research is indicating is the right price.

A good way to do that is to imagine yourself putting your listing on the market tomorrow at, let's say, $239,900, which is in the range your research has indicated is in the ballpark.

Just imagine it...loading up your listing on the MLS at that price with an accurate description and appealing, but realistic photos... and ask yourself, are you excited about it? Do you feel confident that you'll have a few showings right away? Would you show the house to *your* buyer if you had a buyer in that price range for that sort of house? If someone were to call you off your sign and ask about the house, would it be easy for you to "sell" the home to the caller because you truly feel it's priced well? And here's a kicker—if YOU were in the market for a home in this price range in this part of town, would YOU be interested in this home at this price?

Or (dangit) is your gut telling you something different? Are you worrying about the smoke smell? Are you concerned that your seller's requirement for 24-hour showing notice is going to be a problem? Do you worry that the apartment building next door is going to turn buyers off?

Because here's the thing. When you've done your homework AND then you ask your gut how it feels about the price you're considering...you can trust what your gut tells you. Because even if there's a problem with the home—like the examples I just mentioned—when you put the right price on the home to account for the obstacles, you'll still feel good about your ability to sell the property.

Of course, the more experience you have both in working with buyers and in pricing homes, the more knowledgeable your gut may be, but even if you're new, your gut WILL talk to you about what it thinks the right price is, or perhaps more specifically, what it isn't...which will lead you to what it is.

Now, I suppose this is the time where I give you a magic formula to take all of this information and plug it into a spreadsheet which will then spit out the exact right price. But, unfortunately, that's not how it works—at least not in my experience. Oh, sure there ARE programs that will do that for you, but as I've already said once or twice, I don't trust them to do it right. Again...proper pricing is an ART, not a science and that's what makes it fun!

Attribute #5: Photography Skills

Exceptional Real Estate Agents understand the importance of having great photos online and are willing to invest the time and money to either take great photos themselves, or hire someone to do it.

So, first things first. If you know you don't have a knack for real estate photography...or you don't want to invest in a decent camera...or both...commit to using the services of a professional photographer (or even a really good amateur one).

Taking good pictures of my listings was something that came naturally to me, so when I'd see the awful photos on the MLS of other agents' listings, I jumped to the conclusion that these other agents were simply lazy or even...how to say this nicely? On the lower end of the intelligence scale.

But one day my partner (who I knew for a fact was neither lazy nor on the low end of the intelligence scale) went out to take pictures of our new listing and returned with photos that were, at best, mediocre. From then on, photographing our listings was exclusively my domain, but I realized that having a good eye for real estate photography was not something that comes naturally to everyone.

So, if you already have that good eye and are just looking for a few tips—great! I hope this chapter will provide them. If you don't have a good eye, keep reading anyway. If nothing else, you may read something that will be useful to you as you are looking for a real estate photographer to hire.

WHY Photography Skills?

Great photos sell houses.

Well, to be more exact, great photos inspire buyers to want to see the house... and the more buyers who see a house (assuming the reality lives up to the billing, more on this later), the more likely it is to sell! And you know what else? Great photos don't just excite buyers, they get buyer *agents* all revved up as well, thus making the house even more likely to be shown...and thus...sold.

But you know who else is looking at the photos you've posted of your listings? Your potential future sellers! The last time I went looking for a real estate agent to market one of my own properties, the first thing I looked at were the photos displayed of their current listings. I figure that if an agent is too lazy or indifferent to take (and post) great photos, he or she is likely too lazy and indifferent to satisfy me in other ways. But if they impress me with their attention to detail in their listing photos, I'm going to be more inclined to assume that I'll be satisfied by their attention to detail in other matters related to my real estate transaction.

Equipment

Ask a dozen real estate agents what the best camera is for real estate photography and you'll get a dozen different answers. Some swear by their iPhone, some say a decent point-n-shoot does the trick, others proclaim that you must spend hundreds, even thousands of dollars on a fancy-schmantzy camera, lens, flash and tripod.

I fall in with the middle-of-the-road crowd. No, I don't think your iPhone makes the cut, but neither do I think you need to bust the budget on expensive equipment. Most of my real estate photography was done with a medium-quality point-n-shoot and I'm confident that the quality of my photos was acceptable, even Exceptional ☺.

The biggest consideration when selecting a camera for real estate use is that it has a wide angle lens, so start there. While a 28mm lens is technically considered wide-angle, in my experience, it's not wide enough. If you can find one with a lens closer to 24mm, you'll be much happier with the camera's flexibility in tight spaces.

Tips for Taking Exceptionally Bad Real Estate Photos

Before I get to my tips on taking good photos, let's have a little fun at the expense of the real estate photographer-wanna-be's out there who embarrass our industry on a daily basis! (If you want to have some fun, just visit **www.BadMLSPhotos.com**—it's hilarious!

Tip #1: Using your non-wide-angle lens, take pictures of the corners of rooms, demonstrating that the rooms do, indeed, have corners.

Tip #2: Take your exterior photos on the way home from your day job, after dark.

Tip #3: Take pictures of meaningless spaces, such as the small, empty laundry room, highlighting the dryer plug and vent.

Tip #4: Advertise a killer mountain, lake or city view, but don't include any pictures of it.

Tip #5: Stay in your car when taking exterior shots. Your car window will frame the scene nicely!

Okay, that was fun...

...but let's return to BEING Exceptional and taking great photos of your listings.

Tip #1: Take pictures of main rooms from every different angle and eye level you can. You'll be surprised when you get back to the office and download the photos which ones turn out to be your favorites.

Tip #2: Take close-up photos of any interesting details such as vintage hardware, unique light fixtures that will be staying with the home, detailed woodwork or custom tiling.

Tip #3: When photographing bathrooms, be sure the toilet lid is down, and that all clutter and cords are removed from countertops. This sounds obvious, but I can't tell you how many times I got home after a photo shoot and discovered that I'd photographed hair-dryers, toothpaste or acne medicine.

Tip #4: If the home has a special feature that is reflected in the price (e.g., a great view, amazing landscaping, a special setting), be sure to include photos of the feature. When I was shopping for a lakefront property a few years ago, I was amazed how many listings promised lake footage, but didn't have any pictures of it.

Tip #5: Capture the street scene if it's a selling point.

Tip #6: Be sure your main exterior photo is in season (no snowy yards in July!), but feel free to use the seller's photos of other seasons (e.g., beautiful fall colors, full foliage in summer) as supplemental photos.

Tip #7: Look for interesting or unusual angles such as looking down a winding staircase, across a gleaming granite countertop or up to a custom skylight, or a uniquely coffered or beamed ceiling.

Tip #8: Include pictures of nearby amenities such as parks, trendy shopping districts, golf courses, etc.

Wanna have some fun on a beautiful Sunday afternoon? Charge up the camera and head out into the neighborhood where you have a listing already or tend to do a lot of business. Take lots and lots of pictures of the amenities of the area—the parks, the restaurants, the coffee shops, the shopping districts, the Montessori school, even the public transportation depot if that's a selling factor. You'll be able to use your photos over and over, both to advertise your existing and future listings in the area and in your personal marketing to demonstrate your market expertise.

I always kept my camera with me on my day-to-day wanderings just in case I happened across a photo-worthy shot that would make a great addition to my portfolio of neighborhood pictures (e.g., a family of ducks swimming along the shore of an urban lake as the sun was setting).

Should You Photograph Negative Features?

We could probably debate this question for hours! Should your photos reflect only the positive attributes of the home, or should you set reasonable expectations upfront so the buyer and her agent aren't disappointed with the reality?

What if the home sits under high-tension power lines? Or what if it has a structural issue that will likely make a buyer nervous? What if it's on a busy street or next door to an apartment building? Should you include realistic photographs and/or disclose the defects in your marketing?

Personally, I believe you should disclose, either in your photos or written description, or perhaps even both. Here's why.

JENNIFER'S BLOG: Do You Disclose an Obvious Material Defect In Your Marketing?

Many years ago, I had a sweeeet little listing in Denver. A 1940's stucco Tudor, with all the fixtures and features Tudor-philes love—glass doorknobs, art-deco light fixtures, oak floors with inlays, decorative tile window sills, vintage fireplace...it was an easy house to fall in love with.

And buyers did...over and over again. Fell in love, that is...UNTIL...

<key spooky music>

...they reached the back bedroom. Unfortunately, the entire northwest corner of this sweeeeet little stucco Tudor was sinking. Not only did the floor slope alarmingly, there were 1"-2" cracks all along the back wall and across the ceiling.

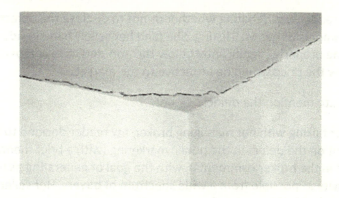

Ouch.

How fast do think buyers ran screaming for the door?

(pretty fast)

Other than the minor issue of a quarter of the house falling off, the home truly was wonderful. It sat on an oversize lot, had a finished basement, an updated kitchen and two full baths and the price was great since we knew we had an objection to overcome. It was staged and photographed beautifully.

BUT WE DIDN'T DISCLOSE THE STRUCTURAL DEFECT IN THE LISTING DESCRIPTION, hoping that buyers would fall so in love with the home, they'd be willing to overlook it.

(Silly, silly Jennifer.)

The house didn't sell. And didn't sell. And didn't sell some more, even though we had scads of showings.

It finally occurred to me that we were attracting the wrong buyer—the adorableness of the house was bringing in the Pottery Barn crowd by the dozens, but...the Pottery Barn crowd ain't much interested in a house with a serious structural issue.

Here's another example.

Recently, one of my readers wrote to me describing a dilemma she was having with a new listing. The home was cute, in a great location, with great square footage and tremendous potential. BUT (sigh—always a "but"), it had a material defect that would likely scare the pants off the majority of retail buyers. The defect was fixable, but at significant cost.

My reader was debating whether or not to disclose the defect in the public comments of her MLS listing. She (and her seller) had already priced the home properly (significantly below the non-defective comps), and she knew the price would be attractive to the market.

But...to mention the defect? Or not...?

After talking with her managing broker, my reader decided to be silent on the defect in the public marketing (with a brief mention of it in the broker comments), with the goal of generating as much activity as possible from a wide spectrum of buyers. Her seller agreed with this approach and away they went.

Well, the strategy worked, sort of. They had a bunch of showings the first week—woo hoo!

But...no offers and universally negative feedback. *"My buyers loved the house until they got to the basement...then...yikes!"*

At the end of seven days, her sellers asked her to change the marketing to more accurately reflect the reality of the situation. They admitted they were tired of all the showings, knowing that most of the buyers wouldn't consider the home at any price, and the negative feedback was wearing them out emotionally. The agent admitted to similar feelings—that she was starting to dread notices of showings and subsequent agent feedback.

So, the agent changed the marketing as requested and immediately was rewarded with two showings, presumably by buyers who were willing to consider dealing with the defect. The agent told me that her enthusiasm level improved dramatically once she felt she was advertising the home more accurately, and felt she'd learned a valuable lesson in marketing—"UNDERpromise and OVERdeliver!"

~ ~

The Moral of the Story? The more realistic your photos are, the less likely buyers will be disappointed with the reality of the home.

Attribute #6: Good Problem-Solving and Negotiating Skills

An Exceptional Real Estate Agent doesn't fall apart and go all drama-queen (or king) when the going gets a little rocky. She stays calm and focused, and tackles problems head-on. She is a skilled, confident negotiator.

If you ask a real estate agent what, specifically, she loves about her job, often the answer will be something along the lines of "*I love helping people achieve their dream of homeownership,*" or "*There's nothing so rewarding as handing a first-time homebuyer the keys to their new home,*" or simply "*I love going to the closing table and collecting that big paycheck for my work!*"

All well and good.

But if you ask ME what I loved about being a real estate agent...my answer is somewhat different. Sure, I liked closing day and had no objection to big paychecks, and I enjoyed helping people achieve their dreams, but truth be told, it ain't what got me up in the morning.

What I LOVED about the practice of real estate was the challenge of solving the seemingly unsolvable problems that inevitably arise during a real estate transaction. To me, there was nothing like the satisfaction of being confronted with a potentially deal-breaking problem, going into temporary panic-mode, THEN settling down, sorting it out, making some phone calls, solving the problem (yahoo!) and moving forward.

And the more often you are successful in overcoming such challenges, the more confidence you have in yourself that you CAN do it—and that is a beautiful thing. When you get That Phone Call with bad news...and you can say to yourself "Well, crap. Crap, crap, crap. Darnit, darnit, darnit! Okay, let's figure it out," knowing you WILL figure it out—it's a powerful feeling.

So how do you get there—how do you get to the point where you don't fall apart when you get That Phone Call?

Adjust Your Attitude

Truthfully, not falling apart and fixing the problem have as much to with your own mindset as with anything else. If you **believe** that you can Solve the Problem, even if you have no idea how you're going to do that, you've already taken a huge step toward making it happen.

But what if you don't believe you can Solve the Problem? Well, this is a rare instance where I will encourage you to Fake it 'til you Make it.

The next time you receive That Phone Call, take a deep breath, smile and say, *"Okay, no big deal. I can fix this. I'm not sure how yet, but I can and I will. I always do."*

Try it now, just for practice. Did your body relax? Did your mind clear? Do you feel just a bit more confident that yes, indeed, you CAN fix any Problem that comes your way? Because...you always do?

Don't Focus on Your Payday

When faced with a potentially deal-breaking Problem, it's natural to immediately think of how a broken deal affects Number One (i.e., YOU). *"Oh crap. I really need this commission check. I'm freaking out now!"*

STOP. While you aren't a bad person for thinking this way, this attitude will only get in the way of your actually Solving the Problem and, yes, preserving your payday. Focus on the PROBLEM, not the financial implications to you. You'll enjoy a far better outcome, I promise.

Calm Down Before Talking to Anyone, Especially Your Client

I'll admit I always struggled with this. As soon as I received That Phone Call, my natural instinct was to call everyone involved and fill them in on the latest catastrophe, including graphic descriptions of the idiocy and incompetence of the third party who created the Problem followed by dire predictions of what might happen next.

Again. STOP. If you need to, take a few minutes (or even an hour) to panic in private, and then take a deep breath, smile and say to yourself, *"I can solve this, I'm not sure how just yet, but I can and I will. I always do. Now, who can help me?"*

Not All Problems Are Yours to Solve

As a buyer or seller representative, we often feel that it's our duty to shoulder the burden of every single challenge that comes along during the course of a real estate transaction. But you know what? That's simply not the case; while others involved in the transaction may happily allow you to take on their

Problems, it is possible to politely, respectfully and gracefully decline to take responsibility for Problems that are not yours to solve.

When you are presented with a Problem that isn't yours to solve, be sympathetic but don't offer your assistance. *"Oh no! What are you going to do?"*

Not All Problems Should be Solved

That said, sometimes a potentially deal-breaking Problem should, yes, break the deal. If, after some calm analysis, you (and your client) determine that the transaction should not move forward, don't fight it. Accept reality and be grateful the Problem stopped the transaction now as opposed to later. Take a moment to (privately) bemoan the delay of your payday, commiserate briefly with your client about the delay of his or her goal and confidently move forward.

Something better is waiting for you both.

Remember—Everyone Wants This to Work!

It's easy to feel as if the "other team" is bound and determined to keep your client from getting what he wants—whether that's the home he's under contract to purchase or the closing of the property she's selling. But remember, in most cases, everyone involved has a stake in getting the transaction to closing—yes, even the opposing team! While there certainly may be plenty of tough-talk and grandstanding during negotiations and, yes, the parties involved each want the best deal they can get, everyone wants the same outcome and is therefore, in a sense, on the same team.

So, as Problems arise, don't assume the other players are hoping for a crash-n-burn outcome. In all likelihood, they'll be delighted to assist you in Getting the Problem Solved.

Okay, so those are tips to keep your attitude in check—how about some solid strategies to SOLVE the dang Problem!?

Can You Throw Money at the Problem to Make It Go Away (aka Do the Math!)

Sometimes it's just easier to open your checkbook and make a Problem go away. Not every time and perhaps not as a first resort, but when you put a dollar value on your time and energy, and realize that writing a check might be the most expeditious resolution, it's worth considering.

Besides, often negotiating parties get so wrapped up in winning the negotiation that they never realize how insignificant the dollar amounts they're fighting over really are!

However, if the dollar amount in question is a bit more than you're comfortable absorbing, propose that all four parties split the bill (buyer, seller and both agents), again, remembering that everyone probably wants this Problem resolved, and when everyone chips in, no one feels taken advantage of.

JENNIFER'S BLOG: Before You Freak, Do the Math!

At the closing of a listing of mine, the buyer's agent was reviewing the settlement statement and noticed that the sales price had been reduced about $1,300, thus reducing the amount she would receive a commission on. She was quite distraught about this and pulled the closing agent out into the hallway to discuss her displeasure (never mind that her buyers were actually paying LESS for the house than they originally thought; therefore, the reduction was good for her client). The closing was held up for 15 minutes while she called her broker to find out what to do.

Ummmm....Do the Math—The difference in her commission check was $36.40 (even less after her split).

A similar situation arose on another listing of mine. The buyers had offered $7,500 above the asking price, with a $7,500 closing cost credit, thus putting the **net** sales price to the seller back at the original list price. I asked the buyer's agent if he minded being paid on the net sales price and he was furious. He said he felt blindsided and that he was counting on that extra commission to buy his clients an extra special closing gift.

Ummmm...Do the Math—The difference in his pre-split commission check was $210 on a total commission of nearly $7,000.

Once I worked with a brand new agent who threatened to terminate her buyer's contract because she forgot to include a rent-back provision in the contract for a 3-day delayed possession after closing. My sellers were under no obligation to pay it and refused to. The new agent declared that her buyers would "walk" if my seller wouldn't pay, so I told her that she was welcome to pay it herself since she's the one who made the mistake. She refused, saying that she couldn't afford to.

Ummmm...Do the Math—It was a $900 monthly mortgage

payment, so a 3-day rent-back would have been less than $90. Hardly a deal-breaker.

My all-time favorite is how real estate agents screamed when gas prices went up to $4/gallon. "We" couldn't afford to work with buyers, couldn't afford to preview houses, couldn't afford to waste our time driving across town to service our listings.

Ummmm...Do the Math—If you drive 300 miles a week showing property and gas prices are $1 higher than they used to be, that's around $15 extra a week you're spending. If you're doing enough business for gas prices to be a significant factor in your profitability, you're doing enough business to absorb it!

~ ~

Ask for Help (but do so with caution)

When a real estate agent, particularly a newer one is presented with a Problem, to whom should she run?

The obvious answer would be "Her broker," right?

Well, yes, in a perfect world. But unfortunately, the real estate industry is far from perfect.

I worked under many brokers during my career and it pains me to say that very few of them were much help to me when Problems arose. Either they were clearly not at all interested in helping me solve my Problem (*"Let me know how that comes out!"*), or their approach was completely contrary to my gut instinct (*"Just tell them to take it or leave it!"*) or, as one of my brokers was fond of advising no matter what the question: *"Tell them to ask their attorney."*

Gee, thanks.

So, even if your broker isn't your go-to person, there are others involved in the transaction who probably can help. For example, if you are having a Problem with the appraisal, ask the lender for suggestions. He's run across this before, probably far more times than you have, and may have some great ideas. If there is an issue with the title work, ask your title officer for help resolving it. If an issue arises related to the homeowners association, contact the HOA president; perhaps they've dealt with it in previous sales.

It sounds obvious, but sometimes we try to solve every Problem that crosses our desk, but you know what? Other people can and WILL step in to help, especially if it's within their area of expertise.

Use Your Team!

As we will discuss in Attribute #7, having a great team of service providers in place is probably the very best way to Solve Problems, particularly during the inspection period, but also throughout (and after) a real estate transaction. For example, how about That Phone Call from your buyer who is moving into the house he just closed on only to discover that the ice-maker water line was disconnected improperly during the seller's move-out and has flooded the kitchen? (Call your handyman!)

Celebrate the Learning Experiences

Try to appreciate the inevitable challenges as they come in. The more challenges you face (and overcome), the more Exceptional of an agent you will be. Further, as you encounter Problems (and hopefully solve many of them), don't let those experiences go to waste! Always take a few minutes to identify the source of the Problem and whether it was something that could have been avoided had you been watching out for it. If so, add it to your checklist! (*Checklist?* Yes, checklist! You'll read more in Attribute #8).

***

Becoming an Exceptional Problem Solver is a process that will develop over time and, in all likelihood, with experience in Solving Problems. So, if you can stand it, be grateful for the Problems that present themselves because with every Problem You Solve, you become a more competent, more professional and more confident real estate practitioner. You may not believe it now, but at some point you might even welcome Those Phone Calls because they give you the opportunity to show off your Problem-Solving skills.

Exceptional Negotiation

Let's move on to Negotiating, which is related to Problem Solving, and many of the suggestions you just read about Problem Solving will apply here as well.

As described in Chapter Ten of my second book, *The More Fun You Have Selling Real Estate, the More Real Estate You Will Sell,* a successful negotiation begins with three caveats:

1. That you respect and acknowledge the intelligence of the guy or gal on the other side of the table
2. That you look for a win/win wherever possible
3. The you strive to see the situation from all perspectives and act accordingly

Now, to be clear, in this chapter we're not going to talk about negotiating for yourself—for your commissions or fees—no, in this chapter we'll be discussing negotiating on behalf of your clients—your buyers and sellers. We will touch on a few ways to negotiate WITH your buyers and sellers, but our focus will be on representing their best interests during a real estate transaction, without creating unnecessary drama, chaos or hurt feelings.

Some agents dread the negotiation process and prefer to avoid it at all costs, while others, conversely, seem to get a rather disconcerting thrill out of making a negotiation as painful as possible for the other side. In this chapter I will share some specific strategies to become more comfortable with the negotiation process, and of course, to maximize the likelihood of getting your client what he or she wants—or as close to it as possible.

Strategy #1: Always Remember Whom You Represent

In most cases, this will be your client—your buyer or seller. Sounds obvious, doesn't it? But I know from (painful) personal experience that it's easy to lose sight of when things get hot and heavy. It's easy to find yourself negotiating FOR yourself (when your deal is trying to fall apart) or even worse, for the other team in an attempt to keep the peace. But of course, if you have an agency relationship with your buyer or seller, it's your contractual duty to represent your client's best interests throughout the negotiation.

But aside from ethical and legal considerations related to remembering whom you represent, simply focusing on your client's best interests makes you a better negotiator. When you take your personal needs, preferences or opinions out of the equation—out of the drama—it gives you more confidence to negotiate from a position of strength.

Focusing on your client's needs will also help you avoid the temptation to bend over backwards in the wrong direction to avoid confrontation with the opposing party. It's much easier to do the right thing when you continually remind yourself WHO, exactly, you represent.

Related to this, always remember WHO is actually negotiating; that would be the buyer and the seller. Period. You and the other agent are NOT parties to the contract and therefore have no power to make decisions on behalf of your clients. As you are facilitating the negotiation, always remember to solicit your client's opinions on how they would like you to proceed—yes, you can and should give them your opinion, but the final decision is theirs to make.

So, as you read the rest of the tips to follow, keep in mind that you should always seek your client's input on negotiation strategy.

Strategy #2: When the Negotiations Get Hot and Heavy—Withdraw

When you're in the middle of a negotiation, whether it's during the original contract negotiation or subsequent negotiations, a great technique is to suddenly withdraw. Silence from your end. Stop communicating with the other side without warning. Overnight at least. Don't inform the other agent that your buyer or seller is going to "sleep on it," just do it.

Why? Because your sudden silence will be very unsettling to the other party. They may wonder if they pushed too hard or too far. They might worry that the buyer found something they liked better or that the seller got word of another offer coming in. They will imagine all sorts of things—none of them good! By the next morning, they may be so worked up they're ready to accept anything that comes from your client, even an offer they countered the day before.

Okay, so maybe it doesn't always work out that way, but you may be surprised at how often it does. However, even if your sudden silence doesn't get you exactly the result you're hoping for, it has the added benefit of giving your client a little space to breathe. And this is a good thing. When negotiations get hot and heavy, it's easy for people to get carried away and agree to a price, term or condition they will regret in the morning. Now you may think this is a good thing—hey, if your client wants to sign a contract, let's get 'er done—but remember whom you represent! It's almost always in your client's best interest not to get carried away in a negotiation, and besides, I'd much rather my client experience remorse *before* they've actually bought or sold something than after they're under contract and want to get out of it, wouldn't you?

Strategy #3: (Almost) Always Counter the Offer

When you receive an offer on your listing, (almost) always counter it. Maybe on the price, but not necessarily if the price is right. If the price is acceptable to your seller, find something else in the offer that needs improvement (and there surely will be something). Maybe the inspection deadline is too far out, maybe the earnest money isn't high enough, maybe the possession date doesn't work for your seller or maybe the buyer is asking for a fixture or appliance your seller doesn't want to include.

Counter *something*. Why?

Because accepting an offer as-is will make the buyer fret that he should have offered less. Should have asked for more. Should have pushed a little harder on this date or that inclusion. But when you counter an offer, even if it's not on price, it gives the buyer the thrill of a successful negotiation and, as described above, wards off any potential buyer's remorse. If you counter on something reasonable and the buyer balks and refuses to sign, it's likely the buyer would have walked at some point later in the transaction, creating all sorts of unnecessary drama. Let's just nip that in the bud.

That said, if the offer you receive is true perfection, if it's obvious the buyer and her agent made a real effort to write you a slam-dunk, you'd-be-crazy-not-to-sign-it offer because they Want That House, go ahead and honor their effort with an accepted-as-written signature. But in most cases in all but the craziest sellers' markets, you can usually find something worth countering.

Strategy #4: Build in a Putz Factor to Help the Other Side Save Face

No one likes to feel bullied or pushed into a corner when negotiating—everyone wants to feel as if they won, or at least scored some points. So, when negotiating, encourage your client to always give something to the other side, even if it's just a little something.

For example, if your seller receives an obnoxiously low offer on her home, she may be tempted to reject it outright or counter back at full price simply to express her displeasure at the perceived insult. And sometimes this is the right thing to do if the buyer is clearly bottom-feeding and your listing isn't bottom-feeder material. But often the buyer is simply testing the waters and is perfectly willing to pay a reasonable price. In this situation, encourage your seller to counter back at a few thousand below asking price and politely deliver the counterproposal to the other agent with a smile and a thank you—no snootiness or apology required!

While the buyer may not be thrilled with the counterproposal, they may very well accept it if they want the home, and won't feel as if they were told they could "take it or leave it."

Here's an example from my own career working with a buyer. During the inspection, we discovered a number of significant issues that my buyer was adamant needed to be corrected or a credit given toward repair. We asked for $2,000 which was a reasonable figure. The seller countered back with $1,000 which wasn't acceptable to my buyer. My buyer wanted to go back at $2,000 with a "take it or we'll walk" message, but I suggested that he ask for $1,800 instead. Which he did, the seller accepted it, and everyone was (more or less) happy to move forward.

Strategy #5: Never Believe It when Someone Says "Bottom Line" or "Highest and Best."

I've said these words myself, many times. "This is my best offer!" or "This is my bottom line—tell them to take it or leave it!"

Guess what? It probably ain't true. It wasn't when I said the words and it probably isn't when your client says them. Which means, guess what? It's not true when the other team says them, either! No one truly knows what their "highest and best" or "bottom line" is until they actually get there. And it's highly likely that whatever that eventual highest-and-best or bottom-line figure is has absolutely no resemblance to any numbers proclaimed even an hour earlier.

Here's an example. An agent friend of mine wrote an offer for her buyer of $400,000 on a home listed at $439,000. The seller countered at $420,000 stating that it was their "bottom line." Because my agent friend's buyers had declared their "highest and best" to be $410,000, my friend sighed, delivered the message to her buyers, who also sighed, and both made plans to hit the road again in search of another home.

I, being the smarty-pantz real estate agent extraordinaire that I like to think I am, suggested she ask her buyers if they'd be willing to counter the counter at $415,000. They excitedly agreed and wrote it up. And guess what? The sellers happily accepted it!

No one knows what the bottom line is until they reach it. Not the listing agent, not the buyer agent, not even the buyer or seller. And chances are that any proclamations of bottom line (or top offer) are thousands of dollars from what the seller would be satisfied taking or the buyer satisfied paying.

As the representative of the buyer or seller in a negotiation, never, ever allow the negotiations to die on your side of the table. Always counter a "final" offer, even if you "know" the parties involved are as low (or high) as they'll go.

Because you don't know. And, frankly, neither do they.

On a related note, I can't tell you how many times I've seen an agent on a real estate reality show push her OWN client to accept an offer or counteroffer because "the other agent says this is their bottom line." Nonsense!

Never, ever advise your buyer or seller client to pay any attention to such proclamations, and push them to accept a "final offer" just to save you the trouble of drafting up yet another counter-offer. If your buyer or seller wants to push a little harder, just write it up! I think you'll be surprised (pleasantly) how many times a "dead" deal will come together if you don't accept anyone's "final offer".

Strategy #6: Don't Ask Your Buyer or Seller for Their Highest and Best or Bottom Line.

On a related note, never ever ever ask your buyer or seller for their Highest & Best or Bottom Line. You do NOT want them uttering those words out loud because once someone has declared their line in the sand, they are committed to that line and may be embarrassed later if they are willing to go beyond it.

And heaven help you if your seller tells you their rock-bottom price and lo and behold, an offer comes in at exactly that price, or conversely, your buyer tells you how high they will go and, yeah, you guessed it, the seller counters their offer at exactly that price. Yeah, I've been there.

What if your buyer or seller client tells you their Highest & Best or Bottom Line without your asking? Ignore it. Pretend you didn't hear them. Don't try to explain why they need to stay flexible, just smile politely and change the subject.

Strategy #7: Always Get It in Writing.

I'll admit, in my heyday I was usually happy to play the oral negotiation game of going back and forth over the phone or email after the offer was presented, fine-tuning the price, terms and other provisions until we reached agreement.

> **THEM:** "Got your offer—my sellers want to counter at $415,000. Will you check with your buyer and see if that will work?"
>
> **US:** "My buyers will come up to $410,000 if the washer and dryer are included. See if that will work."
>
> **THEM:** "The sellers will take $412,000, but want to move the closing date up a week."

US: "Okay, will they include the washer and dryer if we do that?"

THEM: "Let me check."

US: "Yes, they will include the washer and dryer at $412,000."

THEM: "Cool, you want to write it up or shall I?"

Yeah, I did this. But in retrospect, it's a bad idea. Why?

Oh, let me count the reasons…

First, people have lousy memories as to what they agreed to, even if they agreed to it an hour ago! You may swear you heard the agent say they'd include the washer and dryer, but when the seller sees it in writing, she balks and you're back to the negotiating table. Or your buyer changes his mind about the price between the time you deliver the good news of a successful negotiation and the time you ask for his signature on the official document.

It's a much better practice to simply Get It In Writing when negotiating. Keeps everyone on the same page (literally and figuratively!) and at the end of the day may just get the job done faster than all the oral back and forth.

Strategy #8: You Can Say No

This was an eye-opener for me about five years into my career. You can say no (or more specifically, you can advise your client to say no).

I learned this when I was representing a home builder on the sale of a custom home. A potential buyer requested a super-duper gazillion-year home warranty that was going to be difficult to get, not to mention prohibitively expensive. I tried to convince my builder client to agree to the warranty (oops, forgetting who I represented, perhaps!) and he said those magic words…

"Jennifer, you can say no."

Wow, what a concept. We can say no! Which we did, and guess what? The buyer accepted the "no" and we moved on with our negotiation.

The funny thing is, a lot of the time, the other side is fully expecting you to say no; they just feel they have to ask. Or how about this—the buyer or seller on the other side asks their real estate agent to make a ridiculous request, so the agent presents it to you, hoping against hope that your client will say no!

For example, the buyer for one of my listings wanted to move into the home prior to closing (what is known as an "early possession" and is almost always a terrible idea).

The buyer's agent made the request through me and I presented it to my seller with my recommendation to Just Say No, which he did. When I delivered the "bad" news to the buyer's agent, she said, "Thank God"; we both laughed and moved on.

Strategy #9: Make Provisions and Counter Proposals Positive

When writing provisions or counterproposals, try to keep your words positive, not negative. For example, instead of countering a request for the seller to pay for the termite inspection with the phrase: "Seller will not pay for a termite inspection," rework it to say, "Buyer will pay for termite inspection."

Strategy #10: Remember that Everyone in the Transaction Feels Vulnerable

Regardless of any grandstanding or power play negotiating, everyone involved in a real estate transaction feels vulnerable. The buyer is nervous about getting her loan; the seller is worried about buyer's remorse and of course, both agents are hoping for a relatively painless trip to the closing table. Everyone wants this to work! Remember that and it will help you feel more confident and less intimidated while negotiating.

And finally,...

Strategy #11: Choose Your Numbers Wisely

Numbers have power, above and beyond their actual numeric value! How many homes are listed at, say, $299,900 as opposed to $300,000? Is $299,900 significantly less than $300,000? Um, no, but it sure looks lower, doesn't it?

You can use this to your advantage with both buyers and sellers. When working with your seller, structure a pricing counterproposal to look as low as possible to the buyer. Instead of countering an offer at $370,000, counter at $369,900. On the flip side, if you're working with a buyer, advise her to offer $370,000 instead of $369,900!

I had my own home listed for $420,000 and received an offer for $390,000. I called the buyer's agent and (contrary to my advice above!) told her I would be countering at $400,000. She begged me to keep my counter in the $300,000's so I revised my counter to $399,900 and voila! Counter accepted. Hey, sounds trivial, but it really works!

~ ~

JENNIFER'S BLOG: Something Troubling You?

I want you to take a moment...next time you have a free one...and think about something that's bothering you. Something that's worrying you, that's keeping you awake at night, that's always on your mind and bringing you down.

I'm guessing it's pretty easy to do, huh? Not too many of us suffer from a LACK of things to worry about, right!?

Okay, now...voice your worry. Say it out loud.

For example: "I'm worried because I don't have any prospects in the pipeline and don't know where my next client is going to come from."

Or...how about: "I'm so busy right now I can't keep up. I don't know how I'm going to get everything done and I'm scared something is going to fall through the cracks."

Or (from my rescue world): "The shelter is so full and the dogs just keep coming. There's no way we can save them all."

Next step...take that worry statement and turn it into a *believable positive*. For example:

"I don't have any clients right now, but that'll change soon enough. It always does—it always works out even when it seems it won't! I'm not worried."

Or..."I have a lot to do, but somehow it all gets done. I don't know how I do it, but I always come through!"

Or (my favorite rescue mantra): "We make miracles happen every day! I don't know how we do it, but we do!"

Did you notice how different you felt when speaking the worry statement out loud versus the believable positive one? Did your body relax? Did your mind clear? Did you maybe stand up a little straighter and even smile to yourself?

I know I do...when I find myself worrying about something, I try to remember to turn it into a believable positive statement and when I do...the whole world seems brighter. And I feel a sense of power over my troubles that gives me the edge I need to make my believable positive statement a reality!

~ ~

Attribute #7: A Great Team

An Exceptional Real Estate Agent has a great team. If a client needs a referral to a handyman, house-cleaner, structural contractor, roofer or painter, an Exceptional Agent knows who to call.

Want to know one of the very best things you can do for your business?

Get a team in place as fast as you possibly can! I promise you, once you do, you'll wonder how you ever got through a real estate transaction without it. Having a great team will not only make you a much better real estate agent, it will also, to put it bluntly, make you a lot of money.

Well, perhaps it's more accurate to say that a great team will help you RETAIN a lot of money. While having a team doesn't manufacture buyers and sellers for you, once you HAVE buyers and sellers, it will go a long way toward making sure that those buyers and sellers end up at the closing table so that you get to take home a paycheck.

In retrospect, I wish I'd kept track of how many of my transactions were saved by my team. If I had to guess, I'd say, conservatively, at least half of my transactions might have failed if it hadn't been for my team; my handyman, in particular. Actually, I wouldn't be surprised if that number were closer to 75%...or even higher.

I was stunned the first time I hired a listing agent to represent me on an out-of-town property I owned when I asked him for the names of a few contractors to help me get the house ready for market and he had nothing. No one. NO ONE. Not a handyman, not a painter, not a plumbing or HVAC guy. Not even a house cleaner. I was trying to get my house ready to go on the market in an area where I didn't know anyone except my real estate agent and was only in town for a few days. When my agent couldn't recommend anyone, I hit the phone book and came up empty. Guess what happened? The work didn't get done...the house didn't sell... and no one won. And honestly, his credibility with me was shot forever.

But that's only one example of how having a team is good for business. Let's back up a bit and talk about what, exactly, a team is.

Your team consists of reliable and reasonably priced home improvement service providers who help you take care of your buyers and sellers before, during and after their purchase or sale. Your team members do not work exclusively for you in all likelihood; they are independent contractors with whom you have a good relationship, and can depend on to be responsive when you or your clients need their services.

> **NOTE:** in the context of this chapter we're not talking about other people you may consider to be on your team, such as a buyer agent, transaction coordinator, assistant or partner. Nor are we referring to other professionals involved in your real estate transactions such as lenders, inspectors, appraisers, attorneys or title officers.

So who do you need on your team?

First, you need a handyman. No question, if you can only have one team member, that's who it would be, a handyman. Someone who **can do** pretty much anything **and is willing to do** pretty much anything. If, in your first conversation, a handyman leads by telling you all the things he doesn't do, then he's not your guy (or gal). What you want to hear is something along the lines of, "I do pretty much everything you'd need, except roofing and carpet." But if he gives you a long list of things he's not interested in doing, you'll just end up frustrated.

A handyman may not be licensed, bonded or insured, and in most cases that's okay. We'll talk about liability a little later, but your ideal handyman is exactly that—a really handy guy or gal who can fix pretty much anything.

Who else do you need?

Well, next up on the list is probably going to be a good HVAC (Heating, Ventilation and Air Conditioning) guy (and forgive me for calling my contractors "guys" from here on out —I know it's not politically correct). You'll probably want an independent contractor, not a big company that advertises on TV and has a splashy ad in the yellow pages. Big companies may not give you and your clients the attention (or pricing) you deserve.

Your HVAC guy may also do plumbing, which is handy for the times when you need plumbing work done by a licensed contractor and your handyman isn't licensed—although in most cases, your handyman will handle your plumbing repairs for you.

You'll also need a roofer and a good painter. If hardwood floors are common in your market, you'll want a good hardwood floor guy, both for installing and for refinishing floors, and again, probably an independent as opposed to a big company.

If you work a lot with older homes as I did, you may need a structural contractor—someone who actually does structural work, not a structural engineer who just analyzes the structural problem and draws up a solution.

You'll also want a house-cleaner and a home stager if home staging is common in your market.

Oh, and of course, you'll need a licensed plumber and an electrician for the times when your handyman's lack of a license will be an issue, although I can probably count the number of times in my career I had to use a licensed electrician or plumber—my handyman could do Pretty Much Everything... and frankly, he did it better.

In your market there might be other trades you'll need, such a sprinkler repair service, well or septic repair, a pool service or pest control.

So, to summarize, your list of potential team members might include:

- Handyman
- HVAC guy
- Painter
- Roofer
- Structural Contractor
- Plumber
- Electrician
- Flooring guy
- House-cleaner

And maybe a home stager, pool service, well or septic repair, sprinkler repair, pest control...

So, the next obvious question is... where d'ya find all these people?!

Well, here's some good news. If you start with your handyman, he can probably lead you to most of your other team members since handymen also need backup from time to time. And you know what else? Forgive me for being non-PC again, but I've noticed that service contractors, particularly male ones, tend to be highly critical of the work other service contractors do, so if your awesome handyman refers you to someone he likes and trusts, there won't be those little professional spats arising among your team. I'm serious ☺.

Anyway, as of this writing, a great way to find a great handyman is Angie's List (**www.angieslist.com**). If you have an Angie's List network in your market place, you're golden. Buy yourself a membership—it's not expensive—and USE IT. Search the database for handymen, read the reviews, contact a few, see how quickly they get back to you and if they seem interested in working with you.

If you don't have an Angie's List in your market, there are other places to find handymen, although Angie's List is way more fun.

- Your sphere of influence—what a great excuse to connect!
- Other agents—although if they have a great handyman they might want to keep him a secret!
- Other contractors you already know
- Your home stager, if you have one
- Property managers
- Your Facebook friends
- Craigslist
- Classified ads in the newspaper
- Bulletin board at a local hardware store

So let's assume you've found your handyman, what's next? Well, as mentioned earlier, ask your new handyman for references and he might be able to pretty much fill in your list. But you probably want to expand your team beyond your handyman's network, so you can follow the same process for each service provider—access Angie's List, ask your friends for recommendations, etc.

I'm sure you realize this, but your team won't be built in a day and it will never be complete. Throughout your career you'll add people to your team, you'll drop people from your team and team members will often vanish without warning. You'll hear some crazy stories and you'll want to pull your hair out in frustration when a trusted team member poofs, so you will need to always have your antenna up for new team members.

But these realities shouldn't stop you from building your team—yes, your team will be an imperfect bunch and some of them might even smell funny, but again, if you have a good team ON your team, you'll be a far more successful real estate agent than if you don't, warts and smells and all.

A Word about Liability

This seems like as good a time as any to talk about liability.

So, are you potentially liable from a legal perspective if you refer a service provider to a client and it goes poorly? Yep, you very well might be. Referring anyone to anyone else is a risky business as we all know. You'll need to decide for yourself if it's worth it to you to be helpful and make the referral while taking the risk that a referral might go bad. To me, yes it is worth it. As I mentioned, having good service providers has served me to the tune of hundreds of thousands of dollars—literally—in saved commissions and happy customers. So, I'll take the risk of something going bad every once in a while, even if it ends up costing me money.

But you know what? The bigger problem I've had has been my beloved service providers having trouble getting paid by my clients far more than the other way around—my guys and gals show up for work, get it done and then have to chase the homeowner for payment!

Interviewing Your Potential Team Members

So, how should you approach your potential team members; what sorts of things should you ask them during your interview process?

Well, if you're using Angie's List, you can simply submit your request online, describe what you're looking for and see if they want to play. Tell them you're a real estate agent, looking for a handyman (or painter or whatever) to refer to your clients and help you out during your real estate transactions. If they're excited about working with you, they'll respond. If they aren't, they won't.

Should you ask them how much they charge? Sure, but don't be surprised if you don't get a straight answer. Handymen in particular, due to the nature of what they do, can't always tell you how much something is going to cost to fix, although they may tell what their hourly rate is. But that rate may not be all that meaningful depending on how efficient they are and what sorts of things go into that rate. What might be more useful would be to give them an example of a common repair (e.g., a garbage disposal installation) and ask for a non-binding estimate of what they would charge.

Since your handyman is such a critical member of your team, you'll probably want to meet him before referring him, so how about inviting him over to give you some estimates on projects you have around your house? If you're comfortable with him, go ahead and have him do the work. If you aren't thrilled with his look, demeanor or attitude, you can send him on his way and try someone else.

How Your Team Can Help You Be Exceptional

So, how can you USE your team in your day-to-day real estate practice? Oh, my, let us count the ways.

Your Buyers at Inspection

The home inspection can be the most painful day of the entire real estate transaction, can't it? Ugh, everyone goes home feeling worn out, beat up and incapable of coherent thought.

BUT, if you have a great team on your side, you'll pull through even tough inspections far more often than if you don't. For example, let's say that the inspection for your first-time buyer reveals gobs of minor repairs and maintenance issues. Most first-timers tend to panic when they hear the words "electrical" or "plumbing" or, gawd forbid, "asbestos." They envision themselves opening up the phone book, waiting hours on end for a contractor to show up and then emptying out the bank account to pay for the service call. Lather, rinse, repeat for each item the inspector identifies as an "issue."

However, if you can calmly and confidently say, "Not a big deal, we'll put it on the Bob list" (Bob being your awesome handyman), your buyer will likely calm right down and might even beat you to the punch at the next issue that arises by declaring that item to be "on the Bob list!"

Or, conversely, perhaps there is One Big Fat Hairy Problem the inspector identifies; for example, a cracked heat exchanger in the furnace. You see your buyer's eyes widen and can almost feel their gut contracting as they imagine the entire family waking up dead one morning due to carbon monoxide poisoning. *Never fear*, you say, *let's get William out here to take a look and give us an estimate for replacement.*

> **NOTE:** even if the Big Fat Hairy Problem is something the seller will agree to correct, having a great contractor to share with the listing agent will often keep your transaction together if the listing agent doesn't have his or her own team in place.

Your Sellers at the Time of Listing

A little while ago I shared the story of my own experience with an agent who didn't have a team in place to help me, the seller, prepare my home for market. If the best you can do is to send your seller to the phone book to find their own painter, floor refinisher or general handyman, I can almost promise you the work won't get done. But when you can offer up your OWN painter, floor refinisher and handyman, you're golden.

I had a listing once where the seller was, like I was at the time, a single woman with a lot on her plate. Her home needed a substantial number of minor repairs, including drywall work, painting, plumbing, electrical and yard clean-up. She knew the work needed to be done, but didn't think she could afford to hire it out, so bravely declared she'd do it herself. Well, um, I knew that would never happen, so I suggested we invite Bob over on Saturday just to take a look around and give us an estimate.

Very happy ending...Bob got all the work done, for thousands less than she was anticipating and the home sold quickly at a good price.

Your Sellers at Inspection

Earlier we talked about how your team can help your buyer at inspection; well, of course, this applies to your sellers as well! When they get that obnoxiously long laundry list of requested repairs from the buyer and you see their eyes widen, you can go a long way toward calming them down using the same approach you took with your freaked-out buyers—"No big deal, let's get Bob over here to take a look."

Here's the really sweet news, especially when you're dealing with a lot of minor repairs. Buyers (and their agents) almost always overestimate the cost of repairs, sometimes to the tune of thousands of dollars. So if you have a great handyman on your team, he'll likely be able to address most or even all of the items on the buyer's list for far less than the buyer thinks, so you and your seller will come out looking far more generous and cooperative than you really were ☺.

And you know what else? The other agent will come out of the transaction thinking you are a "great agent to work with." And trust me, having that reputation among your peers is a very good thing!

Your Buyers After Closing

Another painful time during a real estate transaction where a team can smooth things over is after your buyer closes and takes possession of her new home. Uh oh. Stuff isn't working! Things are broken! Your buyer panics and thinks she's bought the Money Pit! Not to worry. Your team is ready, willing and able to help her out. Just make the connection, follow-up to see how it went and you'll be the hero of the day.

Promoting Your Team as a Resource to your SOI

And of course, it should go without saying (but I'll say it anyway) that if you have a great team in place, by all means share that good news with your sphere of influence! BE the person who knows people who can Get Things Done.

Attribute #8: Great Systems in Place to Track Transactions

An Exceptional Real Estate Agent has detailed checklists and follow-ups in place so that important activities don't slip through the cracks.

As you probably realize, this chapter is not about having great systems in place to generate leads. No, it's about having great systems to help you stay on top of details and strive to never let anything slip through the cracks.

Contact Management

You're probably already familiar with the concept of a contact management system, which is a program you purchase (either with a monthly subscription or an upfront charge) to help you manage your real estate business. Some of the better-known real estate-specific systems include Top Producer, IXACT Contact, ACT!, REST, Agent Office, Wise Agent and Realty Juggler, although there are dozens more to choose from.

Many contact management systems market themselves as being the be-all and end-all piece of software for a busy real estate agent: doing just about anything and everything you could imagine needing a piece of real estate software to do. Newsletters! Drip Mail Campaigns! Contract Preparation! Showing Service! Market Reports! Websites! IDX! Lead Generation!

However, in my opinion, all those extra bells and whistles don't mean a thing unless the system does two basic things well, Very Well. If it doesn't do these two things Very Well, I don't care what else it does, Very Well or otherwise.

These two things are:

- Managing Your ConTACTS, and
- Managing Your ConTRACTS.

Your "conTACTS" are the people who make up your database, aka, your sphere of influence or SOI. Your "conTRACTS" are your active listings and pending sales.

Managing Your ConTACTS

A good contact management system (let's shorten it to CMS) will allow you to easily and intuitively enter contact information for everyone you know, including data for their spouse, partner, children and other relatives. You should be able to input different last names and individual contact information. It should allow you to track the birthdays of all members and notify you of an upcoming birthday and other special dates you want to acknowledge. It should allow you to categorize your contacts into various groups, and the names of such groups should be fully customizable. It should allow you to include a person in more than one group and sort accordingly. It should allow you to link conTACTS with conTRACTS.

Managing Your ConTRACTS

A good CMS should allow you to create fully customizable transaction checklist templates (also known as action plans or activity plans) to apply to your real estate transactions.

For example, the CMS should make it easy for you to create an "Active Listing Checklist" with all of the to-do's associated with a new listing from Day One to the date it expires or goes under contract. When you get a new listing, you simply apply the Active Listing Checklist template to that contact profile and BAM! You have an auto-populated to-do list for the listing that reminds you to do all those things you need to for the seller, on the day you need to do them.

***

So those are the two things a good CMS must do. All the other bells and whistles are meaningless if the system doesn't do these two things Very Well. I don't care if it creates fancy splashy newsletters, I don't care if it has a gazillion drip campaign emails and marketing letters, I don't care if it creates market analyses or listing presentations, I don't care if it blows my nose for me. If it doesn't do the two things I just described Very Well, it's not a good contact management system.

How do you choose the right CMS for you? Well, that is a big question; one that trips up real estate agents every day! The right system for you will depend on your budget, your preference for an online system versus an installed system, your comfort level in learning new technology and the additional features you deem critical to your business model.

If you'd like to know which contact manager I recommend, you can visit my website at **www.SellwithSoul.com/contact-management** where you'll find my current recommendation as to my favorite system and why I think it's so great.

So, let's leave the subject of contact management for the moment and focus on creating those transaction checklists that will help you be the best thing to ever happen to your clients. We'll return to contact management at the end of the chapter.

Transaction Checklists

Ahhhhh...is there anything more exciting than a checklist?! A transaction checklist even?!

Actually...good checklists can change your career as a real estate professional, and therefore, change your life. And, as with several of the other Eight Attributes of an Exceptional Agent, once you have great checklists in place, you'll wonder how you ever provided Exceptional (not to mention refer-worthy) service without them.

Before we dive into the nuts and bolts of creating your career-changing checklists, let's talk about The Transaction Coordinator —i.e., another person who is charged with managing the details of your transactions, whether the Transaction Coordinator "belongs" to you (as in, your own assistant), is a member of the office staff and serves several agents, or is an independent contractor.

Are you thinking that if you have a Transaction Coordinator that you're off the hook and can skip this chapter? Um, no. Sorry. Even if someone else is in charge of keeping track of the dates and deadlines and to-do's associated with your buyer and seller transactions, it's still your responsibility to ensure that everything gets done in a timely and professional manner.

And, frankly, I believe much of what we get paid to do and certainly much of what makes us Exceptional takes place DURING a real estate transaction, so I always preferred to manage the details of my transactions personally. Even the seemingly minor "administrative" items on your checklists can cause you all kinds of grief if they aren't done properly. Besides, the more in touch with your clients you are, the more fondly they will remember you, assuming, of course, that you are reasonably proficient at managing the details of your transactions. If you aren't, well then, you might be better off with a transaction coordinator, but the point is still valid—even if you aren't actually the one DOING the activities on the checklist, it IS your responsibility to ensure that they get done... and done right.

So, read on.

Checklist Defined
So, what, exactly IS a checklist?

A checklist is a list of all the activities that need to be handled during the course of a transaction, listed in the order in which they need to be done. For example, when you take a new listing, there are things that need to be done **prior** to your listing going onto the MLS, things that need to be done on the day your listing goes onto the MLS, in that first week, the following week, etc. When your buyer goes under contract, there are things you'll need to do that day, the next day and the day after that, as well as in the days leading up to closing.

Some of the activities on your checklists will be things you need to handle personally; others are things you need to ensure others are taking care of.

Many real estate agents will take their checklists to the next level and create activity plans from them to be used with their contact management system (which I highly recommend!). The difference between a "checklist" and an "activity plan" is simply the platform the checklist is on—a "checklist" is typically a list on paper; an activity plan is your checklist uploaded into a computer-based system.

Creating checklists is a never-ending process; your checklists will never be 100% "done." You'll probably tweak your checklists every single time you close (or don't close) a transaction! But we have to start somewhere, so let's!

The Three Checklists

You'll need to create three separate transaction-related checklists: one for active listings, one for listings under contract and one for buyers under contract.

Your **Active Listings** checklist will include all the things you need to handle as a listing agent from the time you get your listing agreement signed by the seller to that glorious day the property goes under contract.

Your **Listing-Under-Contract** checklist will include all the things you need to handle as a listing agent from that glorious day your listing goes under contract through the even more glorious date(s) of closing and possession.

Your **Buyer-Under-Contract** checklist will include all the things you need to handle as the buyer representative from the day your buyer contracts to purchase a home through the date(s) of closing and possession.

The process for creating each checklist is the same; however, each checklist is distinct to the transaction type. In other words, you won't just create your first checklist and then tweak it to work for the other two types.

The Process

The process of creating your three checklists is to:

1. Brainstorm every single thing you can think of that must be handled during the course of that transaction type

  1(a): Take a look at the SWS checklists found in the Appendix for additional ideas, if desired
2. Put your list in chronological order
3. Create your checklist using whatever platform you choose (spreadsheet, Word document, contact manager, etc.)
4. Apply your checklist to your current transactions
5. Fine-tune your checklist throughout your career!

Your Active Listing Checklist

So, let's begin with your Active Listing Checklist.

Step One

Take out a pen and paper (or open a blank document on your computer) and write down/type out every single thing you can think of that you should do (or make sure gets done) from the time your seller signs the listing agreement to the day your listing goes under contract.

Don't worry about putting your list in any particular order, just mentally walk yourself through what needs to happen:

— ...in the days **prior to** going on the market

— ...**on** the day your listing goes on the market

— ...the first few days **after** your listing goes on the market

— ...the first week after your listing goes on the market

— ...a few weeks into the listing period

...and beyond.

Try to come up with at least 30 activities.

> **NOTE:** If you're a relatively new agent, this assignment may be difficult for you, especially if you've never had a listing before. But don't be discouraged, just do your best to think of everything you can that makes sense to you would need to be done before and during the active marketing period of a listing. Who knows? Maybe your lack of experience will result in an even more comprehensive or creative list than someone who's been doing this for ages and might be a little stuck in a rut.

Step One(a)

Take a look at the SWS Active Listing checklist in the Appendix to see if you missed anything you'd like to add.

Step Two

Once you have every single activity you can think of on your list, go ahead and put the activities in chronological order starting with activities you'll do prior to your listing going "live" all the way to the date of contract. To make it less complicated and cumbersome, group your activities by date or time period, as follows:

— Activities to be done **prior to** MLS entry (e.g., take pictures, get seller signatures on all documents)

— Activities to do **on** the date of MLS entry (e.g., install lockbox, put up For Sale sign, provide showing instructions to your showing service, etc.)

— Activities to do one-two days after MLS entry (e.g., schedule open house, deliver signed copies of documents to seller, etc.)

— Activities to do by the end of the first week after MLS entry (e.g., blog about your listing, solicit feedback after showings, etc.)

— And so on...

You don't have to put every single activity in order; just put each in the appropriate time period.

Step Three

Create your Active Listing checklist! Because you'll be tweaking your checklist from time to time, be sure to create it in an easily editable document or platform.

Step Four

The next step is to apply your Active Listing checklist to your active listings. This can be done a few different ways.

You can simply staple a printed copy of the checklist to each listing's file, checking off the items already complete, doing any activities that, oops, you forgot to do and making sure to check the list every day for upcoming activities.

You can also use the checklist to enter all upcoming activities into your planner on the appropriate days they need to be done.

If you use Outlook or something similar, you could use the checklist to create tasks and emailed reminders of the tasks.

Or, as described earlier in this chapter, if you are using a real estate-specific contact management system, you can create an Active Listing checklist template in your system and apply it to each of your currently active listings. We'll discuss this further at the end of this chapter.

Step Five

Your Active Listing checklist will be a constantly evolving document, so be prepared to make changes to it on a regular basis as you go through your transactions and identify new activities to include. This is a good thing! In fact, every time you add an activity to your transaction checklists, the more Exceptional you become ☺.

Your Listing Under Contract Checklist

So, let's duplicate the process to create your Listing Under Contract checklist. I won't march you through the five steps again; we'll just summarize them here:

First, brainstorm your list of activities that need to be handled by the listing agent (you) when your listing goes under contract. Don't worry about putting your list in the exact right order, just mentally walk yourself through what needs to happen:

— ...on the day the contract is executed

— ...the first few days after the contract is executed

— ...the first week after the contract is executed

— ...two weeks after the contract is executed

— ...the week of closing

— ...a few days before closing

— ...the day of closing

— ...after closing

Next, put the activities in chronological order starting with activities you'll do on the date of contract all the way to the date of closing (and beyond). To make it less complicated and cumbersome, group your activities by date or time period, as follows:

- Activities to do on the date of contract (e.g., get the earnest money check, change the status in the MLS, order title work, etc.)
- Activities to do in the first week after the date of contract (e.g., call buyer's lender, pick up the brochure box, get payoff information, etc.)
- Activities to do in the second week after the date of contract (e.g., set the closing, put up SOLD sign, prepare for the appraisal, etc.)
- Activities to do in the week of closing (e.g., confirm seller has arranged cleaning, ensure inspection items are complete, etc.)
- Activities to do a few days before closing (e.g., confirm closing time and place, review the closing statement, etc.)
- Activities to do on the day of closing and right afterwards (e.g., prepare the file for closing, pick up sign and lockbox, change the status on the MLS, etc.)

Next, create your checklist, apply it to your current listings under contract and be prepared to fine-tune it forever and ever!

Your Buyer Under Contract Checklist

First, brainstorm your list of every single thing you can think of that you should do (or make sure gets done) from the time your buyer is under contract/in escrow to the day of closing/settlement (and beyond).

Don't worry about putting your list in the exact right order; just mentally walk yourself through what needs to happen:

- ...on the day the contract is executed
- ...the first few days after the contract is executed
- ...the first week after the contract is executed
- ...two weeks after the contract is executed
- ...the week of closing
- ...a few days before closing
- ...the day of closing
- ...after closing

Next, put the activities in chronological order starting with activities you'll do on the date of contract all the way to the date of closing (and beyond). To make it less complicated and cumbersome, group your activities by date or time period, as follows:

- Activities to do on the date of contract (e.g., deliver earnest money, send contract to lender, etc.)
- Activities to do in the first week after the date of contract (e.g., give inspectors' names to buyer, check in with buyer's lender, advise buyer to research hazard insurance, etc.)
- Activities to do in the second week after the date of contract (e.g., confirm that buyer will attend closing, etc.)
- Activities to do in the week of closing (e.g., schedule walk-thru, ensure inspection items are complete, etc.)
- Activities to do a few days before closing (e.g., confirm closing time and place, review the closing statement, etc.)
- Activities to do on the day of closing and right afterwards (e.g., prepare the file for closing, turn the closed file into the office, call buyer after move-in, etc.)

Next, create your checklist, apply it to your current buyers under contract and be prepared to fine-tune it forever and ever!

Back to Contact Management

As you may have figured out by now, I believe every busy real estate agent should have and use a real estate-specific contact management system to keep track of their listings and pending sales. Once you've experienced the joy of having customized checklists (known as "activity plans" or "action plans") that auto-populate your to-do list every time you open a new transaction, you'll wonder how you ever stayed on top of your business without them.

But are you wondering if you can really afford the additional expense of a contact management system? Especially if you aren't at the point where you are overwhelmed with all the dates, deadlines and to-do's of having multiple transactions going on at once?

"But I Can't Afford a Contact Management System!"

A good real estate-specific contact management system costs money. Not a lot of money, but enough to make it a decision worth giving a little thought to.

The cost can be a sticking point for many agents, especially those who are struggling. I hear it all the time—*"But I can't afford $35/month for a contact management system!"*

$35/month.

Yes, times may be tough. The budget may be tight. Every dollar coming into the household (or not, as the case may be) must be accounted for and spent wisely. I understand that and frankly, I'm impressed with agents who don't just jump on a bandwagon to spend spend spend just 'cause someone told them they should.

BUT

Two things.

First, you should never purchase a system, tool or program that you don't believe will cover its cost, either in hard dollars or by saving you time (with which you can go out and earn some hard dollars). I will never recommend that you purchase anything for your business that won't, at the very least, pay for itself, with the goal, of course, being that it pays for itself many times over.

Second (brace yourself, this might sting a little), you are in business for yourself. You are self-employed. You made the leap of faith into your real estate career knowing (hopefully) that you would no longer be protected by that regular-salaried, benefits-included, vacations-paid J O B you left. Selling real estate professionally is not a hobby. It's not (hopefully) a side gig that you do because you have a little spare time. It's your career; it's your profession. And it's up to YOU and YOU only to invest in the tools you need to be successful. And if you're at the point where $35/month breaks the budget, it might be time to re-evaluate whether or not you're doing the right thing by you and your family by being self-employed.

That said, if you spend $35/month for a contact management system, will you automatically be successful? No, of course not. Especially if you don't use it! Do you HAVE to have Contact Management to survive as a real estate agent? Again, no, not at all. But if you bite the bullet and invest in yourself and your business by committing to a good contact management system, it will change your professional life.

And you should fully expect it to pay for itself, many times over.

How so?

There are two general ways a contact management system pays for itself. The first is by managing your conTACTS and the second by managing your conTRACTS.

Managing Your Contacts

A good contact manager should enable you to create and maintain a database of everyone you know, obviously. But it's what you do with that database that will make you money.

What can you do with your database to make money?

You can remember and acknowledge birthdays of the people you know. You can print out a list of those in your social network and ask two people from that list to lunch every week. You'll have a handy place to enter the contact information of new people you meet and add them to your go-to-lunch-or-coffee activities or send them your monthly mass-email and annual calendar. You can take notes on conversations you've had with friends and acquaintances and set a reminder to follow-up with them in a week or two to "see how it went" (whatever the "it" is).

Simple simple stuff! Yet, without a contact manager, even a rudimentary one, most of these easy, friendly, stay-in-touch activities simply won't get done. And it's highly likely you'll forget all about 90% of the people you're meeting out there in the world...and they'll forget about you. A year goes by...and two...and three...and then you wake up one morning and realize you've lost thousands of dollars in real estate income because you lost touch with most of the people you know, and never followed-up with all those people you've met. You didn't mean to, of course, but without a contact manager, it's tough to do even a marginally good job of keeping track of those Very Important People In Your Life who can send you business.

If you don't have (and use) a contact manager, I'll bet you've lost over $10,000 in potential paychecks every year you've been a real estate agent. Probably more. Probably a lot more.

Managing Your Contracts

The second way a contact management system will pay for itself is by helping you stay on top of your transactions—that is—conTRACT management. And this will pay for itself in multiple ways as well.

When you're on top of your business, your clients are being well-taken care of—and they will notice. When you do the things you promised to do when you promised to do them; when you contact your client with updates before they have to contact you and when you head off problems before they even arise; when you always appear to be on top of their transaction—you'll have yourself one (or a dozen) impressed client(s) who will be delighted to spread the word of your impressiveness to the world.

But what's really sweet about having and using good conTRACT management is that you won't drop the ball—at least, not nearly as often as you might without it. When you have fully customized checklists and action plans keeping you on track, things don't slip through the cracks. And when things don't slip through the cracks, you don't have to open your checkbook to fix problems nearly as often. For example, once I got to pay for a thorough housecleaning on my listing after the seller moved out because he "forgot" to do it. So, my Listing-Under-Contract checklist now includes "Verify that seller has arranged cleaning after move-out."

Another time, I got to write a check because I hadn't verified that the HOA fee advertised in the MLS was correct...and it wasn't. We didn't find out until we were all sitting at the closing table and my buyer was, to put it mildly, annoyed. The listing agent (who made the error) wouldn't 'fess up to his mistake, so it fell to me to make things all better. Which I did, to the tune of over $500. Now, right there on my Buyer-Under-Contract checklist is a line that says "Verify the HOA Fee."

So, the moral of these stories is to assure you that if you commit to using a contact management system in your business, it will pay for itself. Over and over.

I promise.

In Conclusion (of Part 1, that is)

Whew.

If you're still with us, you have just read a lot of material about being a competent, even Exceptional real estate professional.

What are you thinking? Maybe… *"Wow! That sounds like a lot of work, I think I'll just shoot for being average?"* or…*"Wow—that sounds like a lot of fun, I think I'll get started right away?"* … or *"Wow! That sounds like exactly how I already run my real estate practice, I think I'll pat myself on the back and get back to work!"*

Or, maybe a combination of all three—*"Wow, that sounds like a lot of work, but also a lot of fun and I'm already doing some of it, so let's go all the way and be 100% Exceptional!"*

And so, unless your thoughts ran along the lines of *"Wow, too much work, think I'll just be average,"* keep reading. There's more where this came from…

Interlude

We real estate agents long to be respected by the general public. We ache to be considered as worthy of acclaim as our CPA, MD and JD friends. We fuss among ourselves when our clients appear to disrespect our time, our knowledge or, egads, our gasoline.

We claim that even though doctors and lawyers and accountants (oh my!) may have a few more years of education compared to our month (or maybe two) of real estate school, that doesn't mean they are any smarter, more dedicated or more qualified to practice their craft than we real estate agents are to handle one of the most important financial transactions most people will ever make.

But, wander through any real estate forum...flip through any real estate industry-focused magazine, even peruse the conference schedule of the NAR National Convention—most of what you see is advice on how to PROSPECT! More Customers! More Referrals! More Leads!

So back to my opening statement. We want to be respected just like doctors and lawyers and such. But I'll venture to guess that the professional journals, the annual conventions and the online forums of these industries aren't focused on cold-calling techniques, farming campaigns and web-lead generation. I'll bet that their memberships' interests lie more in being BETTER physicians, more KNOWLEDGEABLE lawyers and more COMPETENT veterinarians. While there may be articles or seminars or threads devoted to business development from time to time, something tells me that it's a wee bit more, dare I say it, RESPECTABLE, than what we real estate agents tend to obsess over.

Hey, we all know that doctors and accountants and veterinarians are business-people, too. They, just like us, need a steady stream of business to keep their doors open and their Beemers gassed up. They, like us, need to promote themselves and their services to the public. But somehow, they've managed to do it without being called a salesperson. They are "Professionals."

We real estate agents need to make a choice.

Either we're salespeople, and we accept our role as such. Our job is to prospect, prospect, prospect. We'll leave the details to our assistants who actually might care about the clients we bring in.

Or, we can leave the salesperson persona behind and strive to become trusted advisors who attract business by being competent, knowledgeable and, most of all, PROFESSIONAL!

Welcome to Part II

In Part 1 of this book, you read about what it means to be an Exceptional Real Estate Agent. You read about being competent and knowledgeable. About being an expert. About knowing your stuff and knowing you know your stuff.

Hopefully you've put some of what you read into action already, or are planning to first thing in the morning. Maybe you're planning to get out there and start Mastering Your Market. Or devoting a whole day to becoming more Masterful about your Contracts and Disclosures. Or finally creating those transaction checklists you've been meaning to get to.

Fantastic!

But I'd like to challenge you to take Being Exceptional even further, not only in your own practice of real estate, but to also inspire your Exceptionally minded colleagues to do the same.

Um, Jennifer, what do you mean? Take WHAT further? Inspire my colleagues to do what, exactly?

Ahhhh, glad you asked. That's what we're going to talk about in Part II!

What Is a Real Estate Professional?

In Part II of *The Exceptional Real Estate Agent*, I want to talk about ways to improve not only John & Joan Q. Public's perception of our industry, but also our OWN perceptions WITHIN our industry of what it means to be a real estate professional.

A Professional.

Here are some definitions of "professional" and "professionalism" provided courtesy of my friend Ron Stuart (www.ronstuart.com):

- *The professional provides a personal service rather than simply the entrepreneurial dealing of goods.*
- *There is an independent society that maintains a standard of qualification that attests to the competence of the individual practitioner.*
- *There is a specialized code of conduct enforced by the society designed principally to protect the public.*
- *There is a continual investment made in getting better.*
- *Excellence in client satisfaction is an enforced standard.*

Do these definitions (especially the last one) sound like what you were taught in your corporate real estate training? What you've heard preached at industry conventions and seminars? Like what you've observed in your day-to-day practice of real estate?

Probably not. No, traditional real estate training and theory treats this career much more as a sales gig than a professional endeavor. We attend classes and seminars about "generating leads" and "picking up clients." We are advised to "Prospect First, Service Later" and are assured that Prospecting is Job 1. We memorize scripts, bust objections and employ slick techniques to push our clients off their fences.

In fact, as I am writing this section, I'm following a blog written by another real estate trainer who believes that the reason most real estate agents fail is because they "forget" that their primary duty (to whom?) is to prospect. To paraphrase, the trainer writes: *"The primary task of a real estate agent should be lead generation and every day should be built around lead generating activities. Showing homes and going on listing appointments needs to be done in between or after prospecting."*

As I read the blog, I audibly sighed, loudly enough to wake the sleeping dog at my feet. But even more sigh-worthy than the original blog were the dozens of comments that followed, basically agreeing with the premise that contrary to what a new licensee might have expected when she signed up for real estate school, this really IS first and foremost a sales job where client care is secondary to the all-important task of lead generation.

And yes, the Prospect First approach is one path to financial success in real estate, but it's not the only one. I believe there are two viable paths to a successful career in real estate.

Two Paths to Success

The first path is to be an amazing business-gettin' prospector—that is, someone who loves nothing more than an afternoon of belly-to-belly networking (ugh, that visual gets me every time) and has no qualms dialing for dollars when the pipeline gets a little low.

Real estate agents who are Exceptionally good at prospecting may very well enjoy tremendous success in a real estate career due to their prowess in finding a steady stream of new "leads to convert."

The other path to success is to be Exceptionally good at what you do—that is—to expertly manage the moving pieces and parts of a real estate transaction. To blow your clients away with your meticulous attention to detail, your deft handling of the myriad problems and challenges that inevitably arise and your professional demeanor and expert advice when negotiations get hot and heavy.

Real estate agents who are Exceptionally good at getting their clients through an often difficult process with a minimum of hassle and headache may also enjoy tremendous success in a real estate career, due to their clients' inability to keep their mouths shut about their wonderfulness!

The two paths are likely suited to different personalities. Someone who elects to follow the first path is probably outgoing, gregarious and socially adept; someone we might refer to as a Natural Salesperson.

Those who take the second path might be the more introverted, detail-oriented and introspective among us. Someone we might specifically refer to as NOT a natural salesperson!

But unfortunately many of us who fall into this second category are often pressured to take the first path instead, even though we are likely poorly suited for it and will probably fail miserably (that is, we will fail AND be miserable in the process).

But while there isn't anything morally wrong with the first path, it's not typically the approach that enhances the perceived professionalism of our industry. Yes, it can lead to financial success, and it's possible that the top-producing agents in your market fall into this category, but is this type of real estate practitioner one who:

1) represents our industry in a professional manner and, more importantly,

2) represents his or her clients in the manner they expect and deserve?

Now, of course this is not to say that there aren't naturally outgoing, socially adept agents who are also detail fanatics! I'm sure there are, and if you fall into that category, I'm not talking to you☺. Or, if you're a part of a team and your primary duties are rain-making (i.e., finding clients to serve) and you have a partner whose primary duty is to professionally care for those clients you found, again, I'm not lumping you in with those I consider to be less professional.

Who I am talking to here (or, perhaps better said, talking ABOUT since I doubt anyone who falls into the category I'm about to discuss has made it this far in the book) are those who got into real estate because they delight in the gettin'-business and goin' to closings aspects of the career, but aren't so enamored with what happens in between.

The 80/20 Agent Versus the 20/80 Agent

One of my loyal readers wrote to me in horror after his first day of a training program with his real estate company. He told me that the class was instructed to stand up and chant: "Taking care of existing clients will never take precedence over finding new clients!" Or something pretty close to that.

Ugh.

But, unfortunately, it's a popular notion in real estate circles that one should strive to spend **80%** of one's time prospecting for business and only **20%** serving that business.

Interestingly, in the next breath, the same folks declare that their "service" is worth thousands of dollars.

Now that's funny. Sort of. Well, not really.

Honestly, this attitude literally nauseates me. The proponents of this approach justify their opinion by explaining that since the non-income producing activities a real estate agent "has" to do (specifically client service) are typically the activities that give us the most grief and create the most frustration in our lives, we should spend as little time as possible on them, perhaps even relegate them to the hours of the day when our energy level is the lowest so as not to "waste" our high-energy hours taking care of those pesky clients who have the nerve to want our attention after they've hired us.

Wow.

So, they say, because client service activities are not directly income-producing (although I'll argue that one all day long), they should be the lowest priority on your daily to-do list.

I'd like to challenge the 80/20 crowd to share their business model with their potential clients. To write up a plan outlining their goals and commitments in accordance with the 80/20 philosophy, and then create a mission statement based specifically on that business plan.

Can you imagine how the mission statement created from that business plan might read? Something like: *"Taking care of my current clients will NOT be done until I've run out of energy to search for new ones."* My, how proud they would be to post that on their website, blog and in their listing presentation!

I know I'm preaching to the choir here, but I'm having fun, so let's continue.

So here we are. Our 80/20 agent is following the advice of the Big Name training gurus who proclaim that his primary job is to prospect and that he should vigorously resist the temptation to abandon his daily prospecting when clients call with pesky, administrative, non-income-producing problems to solve.

Let's say that all this focused prospecting is paying off, and an agent is gathering an impressive book of real estate business—five, ten, twenty, forty active buyers and sellers. Bravo!

But, just because the agent now has more clients to serve doesn't add hours to the day, so if he insists (as he's advised to do) on sticking to his 80/20 plan (because it's working so well!), his current clients are obviously going to be receiving smaller and smaller slices of his care and attention.

"But," the 80/20 agent protests, *"if I don't make prospecting a priority in my*

business and I do focus on my current clients, down the road I'll find myself with an empty pipeline and I can't have THAT! So, even if I'd prefer to provide great service to my clients, I can't because I need to ensure that I always have new business coming in."

Well, um...

I'm guessing his current clients wouldn't think much of this argument, especially as they're feeling more and more neglected by the agent who promised them the world in service—and isn't delivering. I'm guessing they aren't singing his praises around the water cooler or at yoga class. I'm thinking that if they knew ahead of time that his business model was predicated on spending the vast majority of his time searching for, preparing for and pitching to his future clients instead of taking care of THEM, his current clients, they might have thought twice about hiring him in the first place.

Here's the thing. Taking proper care of clients takes time and yes, energy. A need for a full pipeline doesn't change the fact that our 80/20 agent made promises and commitments to the buyers and sellers who believed he would take great care of them and their real estate needs. Believe me, they did NOT hire him because they were impressed by his prospecting prowess; they hired him because he assured them he'd take better care of them than any of the other agents they considered honoring with their business.

The bottom line is that if you can't handle more than X number of active buyers and sellers without sacrificing your service to them, then I guess you shouldn't be looking for more business when you already have as much as you can properly take care of.

Now let's return to a statement I made earlier—about those agents who, in one breath, poo-poo the importance of client service, but in the next proclaim that their "service" is worth thousands of dollars.

If our 80/20 agent is only devoting a few hours or even a few minutes a week to his clients, don't you think they might start to wonder what on earth they're paying him so much money for? And IF WHAT HE DOES FOR HIS CLIENTS IS SO EASY THAT IT ONLY TAKES 20% OF HIS TIME OR HE CAN HAND IT OFF TO A $12/HOUR ASSISTANT, are his services really worth the fees he charges?

We can't have it both ways. We can't say, on one hand, that client care is simply a collection of administrative tasks that can be handled in our spare time or by an assistant, and THEN in the next declare that our client-care services are extremely valuable and should be well-compensated.

How About a 20/80 Plan?

So how about this? How about we turn that 80/20 philosophy around and strive for a 20/80 business model? Where we spend 20% of our time in search of clients to serve and 80% of our time actually serving them?

Of course, if you are a new or struggling real estate agent and don't have any (or many) clients to care for, then I suppose you should be spending some significant time looking for some—in other words, you probably can't fill up all or most of your working hours serving the clients you don't yet have. HOWEVER...if you hold true to the philosophy of putting clients first—if when you get up in the morning, you make darn sure that your current clients and prospects are fully taken care of before you even think about prospecting, it will pay off for you big time in the future. I promise.

Because you know what? Taking great care of the clients you have is a FANTASTIC prospecting strategy. Those who neglect their current clients so they can pursue their future ones darn well better enjoy that pursuit because they'll be doing it their entire careers. In other words, very few referrals cometh to agents who don't take good care of their clients when they have them.

But maybe that's okay for the 80/20 crowd. Maybe they're so awesome at prospecting they don't need the trust, affection and referrals of their current and past clients, so it doesn't matter if their clients don't think much of them during and after their time together. Maybe the 80/20's are happy to spend their careers devoting 80% of their time to prospecting!

***

How do you feel about the 80/20 versus the 20/80 debate? I hope you fall on "our" side and realize that by being an Exceptional Real Estate Agent who prioritizes client care over client pursuit, your professionalism will be noticed, appreciated and yes, rewarded.

So now, I'll share some ways you can assure that the real estate persona you project to the world is, indeed, professional, dignified and refer-worthy!

How To Be a Real Estate Professional

Strategy #1: Prioritize Your Current Clients Over Your Future Ones

Okay, okay, so we just talked about this for several pages! But it's so important I couldn't leave it off my list of strategies. Besides, I thought you'd like to read my thoughts on what, exactly, "prioritizing your current clients" looks like.

It's easy!

First, obviously, ignore any well-intentioned (?) advice to the contrary. If your broker or trainer insists you follow the Prospect First approach, smile politely and go about your business. No need to argue or debate the issue; you won't change anyone's mind (believe me, I've tried).

When you sit down at your desk every morning, take a look at your client files. Go through each one and ask yourself if there's something that client needs (or would appreciate) from you today. Did you promise to get back to them with some information and (oops) haven't yet? Is there a deadline approaching you need to remind them of? Is there something you did for them recently you want to make sure they are aware of (e.g., previewing a new competing listing or fluffing & flushing[4] at their vacant listing)? Or perhaps, it's just time for a call or note to say, "Nothing new, anything I can do for you?"

As you're making your daily to-do list, make sure to include the client-service items you came up with, and tackle them first. If there are also prospecting activities on your list, that's fine, but they can wait until your clients are all happily tucked in bed (so to speak).

But if, as you're going about your day, a client calls and (egads!) disrupts your prospecting, by all means let it go to voicemail!

JUST KIDDING! Take the call or return it as soon as you can. No prospecting you'll ever do takes the place of having a database full of Satisfied Past Clients. And the secret to building a database of Satisfied Past Clients is to take great care of those clients when they ARE your clients.

Strategy #2: Watch Your Language

We aren't talking about four-letter words here, although hopefully it goes without saying that your appearance of professionalism will suffer if you toss them around like a drunken college student. No, we're talking about the words you use when you talk about your real estate career.

In our industry, as in any, we have a lot of words we use to describe the stuff we

> [4]Fluffing & Flushing: The act of checking on your vacant listings to ensure that everything is as it should be and making any corrections necessary (including flushing the toilets!).

do and the people we do it to. Of course, we "sell" real estate. We "list" houses, we pursue "expireds" and "FSBO's" and we advertise for "buyers" and "sellers."

We promote ourselves as a "Top Producer," a "Multi-Million-Dollar Producer" and the "Top Salesperson of the Year."

We brag on Facebook about the "offers we write" and how we're crossing our fingers that the "deal closes" because we could sure use that "commission check."

In our more private conversations, we debate the best strategies to "capture" and then "convert leads," to "push our buyers off the fence," and to "talk our sellers down on price." We accuse our "buyers of being liars" and refuse to "put them in our car" until they've signed a buyer agency agreement.

Oh, ack!

When you think of yourself as a professional, your language changes, and with that, your behavior toward your clients and potential clients.

For example, you don't "sell" real estate; you "practice" real estate. You don't "list homes," you "market homes." You don't "pursue expireds," you "help frustrated sellers achieve a better outcome." Instead of getting a "commission check," you are paid a "fee."

You don't brag on Facebook about the "deal you closed," you congratulate your client on their new home. You don't strive to "capture" or "convert leads," you "find clients to serve." Your buyers aren't liars; they're just perfectly nice people who need help sorting through their options and identifying the right home for their circumstances.

My friend and fellow professional Ron Stuart says it beautifully: *I've gotten away from thinking like a salesperson. I don't see people as targets anymore; I use a different vocabulary. I don't say 'I sold that home,' but rather, 'I helped somebody buy it.' There's a big difference between selling someone something and helping them buy wisely.*

When I talk about my business, I speak of it as my practice because other professionals speak of what they do as a practice. I don't charge a commission, I am paid a fee. I'm trying to get in a different space from salespeople—commissions are associated with salespeople; fees are more associated with professionals.

Is all of this simply a meaningless exercise in semantics? No, it's not. When you speak differently, you think differently and therefore, behave differently. Stop talking about yourself as a top-producing real estate salesperson who lists and sells homes for a commission check and start talking about yourself as a competent, professional practitioner of real estate who helps clients achieve their goals, and see if you feel the difference!

Strategy #3: Advise, Don't Sell

Contrary to what it might say on your real estate license or your business cards, you are NOT a salesperson. You don't sell anything, except yourself, which is exactly what every other self-employed person on the planet has to do.

No, as a licensed real estate agent, your job is to expertly guide your clients through a complicated process with many moving pieces and parts with the goal of getting them the result they desire. As a professional, you are expected to have the knowledge, expertise and resources to manage a real estate transaction, and further, do so in the best interests of your CLIENT, not the best interests of your PAYCHECK.

Problem is, the way we are traditionally compensated makes this somewhat difficult to do at times, especially when the best course of action for our client puts our paycheck in jeopardy. That's a soapbox for a different chapter (keep reading!), but like it or not, it is your moral, ethical and contractual duty to competently *advise* your clients with THEIR end goal in mind as opposed to *selling* them on a course of action that primarily benefits you.

So, what does it look like, exactly, to *advise* a client as opposed to *selling* them?

An Advisor helps a potential first-time homebuyer decide if now is the right time for him to become a homeowner, while...
...a Salesperson looks for ways to push him off the fence.

An Advisor helps a homeowner evaluate the market and her current situation to determine if now is the right time for her to sell, while...
...a Salesperson uses memorized scripts to convince her to list NOW.

An Advisor meets with the owner of an expired listing with the goal of "figuring out what went wrong," while...
...a Salesperson meets with the owner of an expired listing with the goal of figuring out how to get a signature on the listing agreement.

An Advisor asks questions and really listens to the answers, while...
...a Salesperson pitches and presents.

An Advisor builds her business on the good will of her Very Satisfied Past

Clients, while...
...a Salesperson dials for dollars instead of caring for clients.

Y'know what? I bet that as you read the examples above, you nodded in agreement, perhaps even with a "well, duh" look on your face. Y'know why? Because those who are attracted to the SWS approach to doing business naturally take an advisory approach with clients because, as we like to say, we want to be the best thing to ever happen to our clients.

When we work with our clients, we SWS'ers do so as someone whose goal is truly to help those clients reach their goals, not as a salesperson who is primarily concerned with bringing in a paycheck as quickly as possible.

The good news is, when you approach your clients with a sincere desire to help them, paychecks most definitely cometh quickly!

Strategy #4: Be Honest—Would Your Marketing Work on YOU?

Your typical real estate agent self-promotion is, frankly, dreadful. Ridiculous taglines that would sooner inspire the reader to groan and roll their eyes than to smile and pick up the phone. I mean, seriously? "I'm a SOLD Man!" "Everything I Touch Turns to SOLD!" and everyone's favorite, "I <heart> Referrals!"

But professional-grade personal marketing goes beyond simply striving for non-eye-roll-inspiring taglines. Even if your marketing isn't really cheesy, there's a good chance it's...well...boring (sorry). Or, as we say around here "Dorky[5]"

How can you tell if your marketing is, egads, cheesy and ridiculous, or even boring and dorky?

Easy!

Just ask yourself if the marketing, promotion or advertising you're considering would "work on you." If, let's say, an insurance agent or financial planner marketed, promoted or advertised their service to you in the manner you are contemplating, would it inspire you to:

1. Roll your eyes and think, "This guy's an idiot," or
2. Think nothing at all and toss it/disregard it/forget it, or

   [5]Dorky: Written communication used primarily in self-promotion, which is dry, dull, boring and predictable.

3. Smile, think of the sender fondly and consider giving him a call?

(Hopefully the correct response is obvious.)

As mentioned earlier, this is not a book about prospecting for real estate business, so I won't elaborate here about marketing strategy, but it is discussed in much more detail in my book *Prospect with Soul for Real Estate Agents*.

Strategy #5: Stop Negotiating Your Fee (but no, you don't have to charge everyone the same)

We all know that real estate commissions are negotiable and there is no industry-standard commission percentage that all real estate licensees agree to or must abide by. That said, an individual agent or firm may certainly set their own commission standards and refuse to negotiate from them; there's nothing in the world wrong with that.

Commission negotiation is considered by some practitioners to be an art; a game even. Agents go into listing presentations armed with all the reasons they Won't Reduce Their Commission (how dare you even ask?), ready to whip out their lists of the 154 things they do to earn their breath-taking fee, prepared to tear up a dollar bill to demonstrate how little they get at the end of the day or simply using that tired old phrase "If I can't stay strong negotiating WITH you, how well do you think I'll negotiate FOR you?"

Or, of course, the agent simply folds under the pressure of a seller to reduce his fee when he learns he's competing for the listing.

Ugh. None of these approaches is professional, in my humble opinion.

So, Smarty-Pantz Jennifer, how do YOU recommend we handle the fee, "in your humble opinion"?

Happy to share!

Here's what I think.

I believe it shows an incredible lack of integrity to reduce your fee only for those who ask you to do it, while "holding firm" for those who don't. I mean, seriously? To reward those who are brave enough to request a lower fee therefore punishing those who aren't?

However, I also believe it's insulting and condescending (and therefore unprofessional) to use tricks and techniques to survive the fee negotiation if said tricks and techniques are delivered with the intent to make the client feel guilty for asking.

Hey, there is nothing in the world wrong with asking a professional to justify their fee. That's not being obnoxious; it's being a responsible consumer! Shoot, I'm guessing every real estate agent on the planet who has ever used any of the tried & trite commission-ectomy-avoiding techniques asks for discounts and concessions on a regular basis in their own lives as consumers!

Again, nothing wrong with that and I don't begrudge a real estate consumer's right to push the issue with an agent in hopes of getting a straight, honest and persuasive answer.

So what might that answer look like?

Well, I believe there are two big picture approaches to fee-setting (and therefore, fee "negotiation") that fall under the category of "professional."

Approach #1: Set Your Fee and Stick to It
Whether your real estate fee is commission based or flat-fee based (yes, there are plenty of viable models that are not commission based), set a fee you feel confident about and don't negotiate it. Period. "My fee is X to provide Y service."

When you feel that your fee is a good value for the price; that is, that your client is getting more in value than you are taking in payment (a la Bob Burg and John David Mann's extraordinary book *The Go-Giver*), you will have no qualms presenting your fee and sticking to it.

If pressured to reduce your fee "just 'cause" you can respond with (courtesy of Jackie Leavenworth, the Real Estate Whisperer): *"No, but thank you for asking. I used to reduce my fee, but found that it didn't work for me."* When the seller asks why, she explains that what sellers want most is an agent with integrity and charging less for one person than another would jeopardize that integrity.

Approach #2: Customize Your Fee to Every Transaction
Personally, this approach makes far more sense to me and seems much more professional, especially when compared to the traditional model of charging a percentage of the price of the home bought or sold. I have NEVER heard a persuasive explanation for why the appropriate fee paid to a real estate agent has anything at all to do with the price of the property except that "that's the way it is."

So, it makes sense to me that a real estate agent could (and should) evaluate the apparent degree of difficulty of each individual real estate transaction and set her fee accordingly. Some homes are easier to sell than others. Some buyers will be easier to satisfy than others. Some situations are clearly going to be more labor-intensive and/or risky than others (for example, a buyer with a home-sale contingency or a seller who is underwater on his mortgage). A highly motivated buyer or seller might justify a lower fee than a buyer or seller who is simply kicking tires or testing the market.

Of course, I'm not so naïve that I believe you can predict how easy or difficult a transaction is going to be with 100% accuracy, but other professionals operate in this manner and it works for them. A general contractor gives a binding estimate on a home improvement project and a web developer provides a bid to build a custom website. And if you have the flexibility within your practice to create service packages, you might consider offering combinations of commission + fee alternatives.

Speaking of, I do realize that your managing broker may not be open to your charging customized fees, especially if you attempt to incorporate non-commission based compensation[6] into your practice.

But it's something to think about.

Strategy #6: Don't Memorize Scripts, Have Conversations

Real estate agents are obsessed with scripts. Scripts for every imaginable situation they might find themselves in with a client or potential client from the initial contact to getting an agency agreement signed to discussing list price to agreeing to a price reduction to responding to an inspection request…shoot I'm surprised there aren't scripts out there to help agents deliver a closing gift! (Hold on, gonna check on that. Whew, didn't find any.)

Okay, so I get it that a newer agent might be nervous about having a conversation with a prospect or client that they've never had before, but is the solution to memorize someone else's words to get you through it? Say it isn't so!

(It's not.)

---

[6]This is discussed further in a Bonus section in the Appendix and in great detail in the Accredited Consultant in Real Estate® program at **www.TheConsultingProfessional.com.**

I don't know about you, but when I seek out the services of a professional, I fully expect that professional to be able to TALK intelligently with me about their area of expertise. Call me crazy, but I think a CPA should be able to answer my questions about my personal tax situation as it relates to my desire to rescue shelter dogs without becoming a non-profit. I think my chiropractor should be able to discuss my lower back pain as it relates to the slip-on-the-ice I took last week. I expect my dog-trainer to focus on MY dog(s) and provide individualized solutions to the problems I describe. And yes, I would expect my real estate agent to be able to have a conversation with me about my real estate needs without resorting to memorized scripts or dialogues.

"But, Jennifer," the new agent protests, "*what if I don't know what to say? What if I'm clueless about how to assess and provide solutions to a potential client's real estate needs?*"

Well, um. Hmmmm.

This is where I hope I don't hurt anyone's feelings and this really isn't the place to pontificate on the abysmal rookie training in the real estate industry, but the solution to being clueless is NOT memorizing scripts and dialogues! No, the solution is to become UNclueless as quickly as possible through a combination of reading, training, mentoring and shadowing. (And a good place to start might be Part 1 of this book.)

Okay, so fine, but how about the protestations of the experienced agents who say, "*Just because I use a script doesn't mean I don't know what I'm doing. It just means I say the same thing over and over again in a similar situation.*"

True enough.

But using the same words to explain or discuss something you explain or discuss frequently isn't the same thing as memorizing scripts and dialogues to replace natural conversation. When I refer to someone as a professional (who doesn't need a script!) I'm talking about someone who is able to expertly consult with their clients (and potential clients) depending on their unique circumstances, which is explored *via a conversation*.

Think about this. We all get frustrated with those Level 1 customer service representatives at the cable or cell phone company who clearly have no clue how the system works, but are relying on scripts to solve our problem *("Is the device turned on?")*. However, if, after we've walked through the rep's script, our TV or cell phone still doesn't work, we are referred to a Level 2 or 3 technical support person, who actually understands the system and how to diagnose it using a CONVERSATION.

Anyway, if you want to be perceived as a professional, toss the whole notion of scripts and dialogues out the window and focus your attention on listening[7] to the client and responding intelligently. Besides being more professional, it's also a lot more fun, don't you think?

Strategy #7: Guide, Don't Push

Strategy #7 is to strive to always "guide" your clients toward the right decisions, not push them there.

What's the difference?

Oh, my, where do I start?

How about with a definition of "Guide?"

For our purposes here, we will define "guide" as helping your clients identify and evaluate their options, with gentle and subtle nudges (when appropriate, keep reading) toward the option you feel is truly best for them.

Because, here's the thing. As the expert, as someone who has done this a time or two before, you probably do have a better understanding of the Big Picture and how to best get your clients to the outcome they are hoping for. However, simply pushing your client in the direction you feel they should go won't work. It just won't. People don't like to be pushed and will tend to push back, digging in their heels even when they may subconsciously know you're right.

That's where guiding comes in.

But before I get to that, I must share one important caveat. When guiding your client toward the right decision for him, your intentions must be pure. You must truly want the best outcome for your client, even if that outcome puts your paycheck in jeopardy. If concerns about whether or not you will be paid enter your mind, it will be very difficult for you to properly guide your client. Now, don't be offended; trust me, we've ALL been there and done that! Any real estate agent who says they haven't is lying!

---

[7] By the way, the more you *listen* to your client, the more intelligent and interesting your client will perceive you to be!

But here's the great news. When you truly put your clients' needs first, even at the risk of delaying your own payday, you will reap the rewards of your clients' trust many times over. And you will be rewarded for doing the right thing, I promise. Maybe not as soon as you'd planned on, but soon enough...and often enough.

Let's start with a few ground rules:

Ground Rule #1

As mentioned above, always always always put your clients' interests first—unless you are able to do this, you won't be effective in helping your clients make good decisions and what's more, your clients will feel it. They won't trust you, even if they aren't sure exactly why, and you know what they'll do? They'll dig in their heels on whatever opinion they have and won't be willing to consider your advice, even if deep down they suspect you might be right.

If your client has any suspicion that you are putting your potential paycheck ahead of his or her best interest, your advice will likely be discounted as self-serving. And then no one wins.

Ground Rule #2

(Almost) always take your client's side. Even if you don't whole-heartedly agree with your client's position, I can promise you that arguing with him about his position isn't going to change it—again, he'll probably just become *more committed* to his position if you try to talk him out of it.

For example, when guiding your seller in responding to a lengthy inspection request, you might say: *"Yes, this is quite a laundry list of repairs! Jeez, are they expecting the house to be perfect? Okay, let's see what we have here and what is reasonable to agree to."*

Or when talking with your seller about an unreasonable lowball offer: *"I know, seriously? Obviously they're just hoping you're desperate. Let's draft up a counterproposal and see if they're serious or just fishing."*

Or when your buyer wants to make an unreasonable lowball offer: *"Okay, let's write it up. You never know what the seller will consider!"*

I know, I know, you're mentally arguing with me here that you shouldn't "allow" your clients to run the show; after all, didn't they hire you for your expert advice and "guidance"?

Yep. And part of being a good "guide" is to avoid alienating your client.

Ground Rule #3

When talking with your clients, use the words "we," "our," "us" and "let's." This puts you on the same team as your client, both in your mind and in theirs, which is incredibly powerful. Try it now and see.

"**Let's** try this price for a week and if **we** don't get the activity **we're** hoping for, **we'll** reduce it to $xxx,xxx."

"**Let's** get Bob over here to give **us** a price to repair the leak under the sink."

So, those are the ground rules: Put your clients' interests first, (almost) always take your clients' sides and use words like "let's," "we," "our," and "us."

Reverse Psychology

Reverse Psychology*: A persuasion technique involving the false advocacy of a belief or behavior contrary to the belief or behavior that is actually being advocated. This technique relies on the psychological phenomenon of reactance, in which a person has a negative emotional response in reaction to being persuaded, and thus chooses the option that is being advocated against.*

On the surface, the use of reverse psychology sounds a bit manipulative, doesn't it? Intentionally advocating a course of action that is the opposite of what you actually want to happen, in hopes that your audience will resist your advice and do what it is you actually want them to do?!

And yes, reverse psychology can certainly be used for evil in the hands of an UN-Soulful real estate agent. But when employed WITH soul, it can be a powerful technique to guide your clients toward the best solution or situation for them.

Allow me to explain.

As Bob Burg describes in his excellent book, *Adversaries into Allies*, giving a potential adversary (defined by Mr. Burg as anyone who stands in the way of your personal satisfaction) a "back door" will often result in their having no desire to use it. People don't like to feel pressured to behave or respond in a certain way, so by giving them an out (and the bigger the "out" the better) they are able to mentally relax and evaluate their options. In many cases, they will arrive at the right decision without your pushing it on them or even suggesting it.

Here are some examples from the real world of real estate:

"You aren't going to buy a house today probably. Today is just a fishing expedition to help familiarize you with what's available in your price range."

"I have all the time in the world for you. We'll look at as many homes as necessary to find you the right one."

"No rush on signing a buyer agency agreement. We'll figure out soon enough if we want to work together."

"I don't have a crystal ball and I don't want to give your money away, so let's try $xxx,xxx for a week or so and see how the market responds."

"I may or may not be the right agent for you, so let's just chat for a while and see!"

"Selling a home isn't rocket science, so if you choose to do it yourself, I'm sure you'll be able to."

"It's totally your choice whether or not to reduce the price on your house."

"Of course you can say no to these requests!"

"We don't have to list your home today—when you're ready, I'll be ready!"

I KNOW some of you are gasping at these examples of providing an "out" or "back door" to your clients—I mean, seriously? Allowing a seller to overprice her home? Telling a FSBO that he'll have no problem selling his home on his own? Assuring your buyer that you'll look at 100 homes if that's what it's going to take?

Seriously?

Yes, ma'am. Just try it. I think you'll like it ☺.

Busting Objections

Ugh.

Is there anything more rewarding than overcoming (aka busting) your clients' objections?

Don't get me started.

(Too late.)

Okay, here's what you're supposed to do. Your client or prospective client is questioning whether or not a home (or list price or offer price or whatever) is right for him. In all likelihood, his "objection" is perfectly reasonable, but, egads, it conflicts with his real estate agent's desire for a quick sale/signed listing agreement/whatever and therefore...must be OVERCOME aka BUSTED!

But never fear, there are scads of objection-busting scripts and strategies out there for your objection-busting enjoyment; all of which are guaranteed to convince your client that he is WRONG and you are RIGHT! And that's what it's all about, RIGHT?

Ugh.

Not so much. First, no one appreciates being argued with, especially when the goal of the argue-ER is to convince the argue-EE that he is WRONG. And to compound the insult using tired old scripts and dialogues to accomplish said goal.

That's just rude. And besides that, ineffective.

As Dave Ramsey likes to say, "Those convinced against their will are of the same opinion still."

But perhaps a more compelling reason to throw the concept of objection-busting out the window is because quite often an "objection" is actually a buying sign.

Think about it. If someone has zero interest in a product or service (for our purposes here, let's use the example of a home for sale), they aren't likely to point out what's wrong with it because they don't care. They're already NEXTING that home hoping something more suitable is on the agenda. For example, if the agent shows her buyer a one bath home and the buyer Must Have at least two baths, she probably won't comment on the shag carpet, the dated countertops or the small closet in the master bedroom, except to make conversation.

However, if the buyer is digging the home BUT comments on the location of the master bedroom or the lack of a pantry, all the while continuing to take in the other features of the home—she's INTERESTED!

So, is NOW when you jump in with your handy-dandy objection busters?

NO!

Absolutely not! No!

No, no, no!

Why on earth not? Isn't it your duty as the real estate professional to convince her that her objections are invalid so that she'll race for the offer table and write 'er up?

NO.

Last year my husband and I were half-heartedly looking for a home. We had some rather specific Must Haves and were a real estate agent's nightmare—not terribly motivated and with a home to sell that wasn't on the market. Shoot, we hadn't even spoken with a lender yet. But anyway...out we went to look at homes.

Our real estate agent showed us a home that rang almost all the bells for us. The right price, the right square footage, the right lot size (our hot buttons). However, as we were walking through it, we commented on the location of the master bedroom and the small pantry, as well as the remote location, which was just a bit farther from town than we were comfortable with.

As I made these comments to my husband, within earshot of my agent, I realized I was bracing myself for her to jump in and talk me out of my concern about the master bedroom being right off the kitchen and to point out that there was plenty of cabinet space, just not much of a pantry.

But...what's this? NO objection-busting cometh from my agent! She actually nodded and agreed with us, and went about her business, leaving us to reach our own conclusions.

So, did my husband and I pack up and demand to leave the premises immediately in search of the perfect property with a more-private master bedroom and pantry-to-die-for?

Not at all. We evaluated the situation, decided the two flaws were not deal-breakers and continued our tour of the home. As it turns out, the location of the home WAS a deal-breaker and for the record, as of this writing, we are still living in our modest house in the Panhandle of Florida.

Anyway, my point is that your clients (in all likelihood) are not stupid and do not need your assistance overcoming their reasonable objections. If they want your input, they'll ask for it, in which case you are free to give it, keeping in mind that Arguing Will Likely Get You No Where.

One Final Rant Before We Conclude…

"Lead generation is what selling real estate is all about, plain and simple."

"I have three jobs: Getting a listing appointment, preparing for a listing appointment, and going on a listing appointment.,"

"My primary duty is to prospect. Everything else is secondary."

(These are direct quotes from real estate agents on a popular real estate forum.)

Seriously? SERIOUSLY?

That's why we have to go to real estate school and pass a proficiency test? That's why we have a license and continuing education requirements? That's why we pursue various advanced certifications and designations?

Because selling real estate is "all about lead generation"?

My friends, generating leads is a necessary part of any small-business owner's business model. Whether you're a massage therapist, a dog-groomer, an insurance agent, a dentist, a chiropractor or a real estate agent, you need incoming customers to stay afloat. And it's up to you to figure out how to find those customers and do what it takes to inspire them to hire you.

But that doesn't mean it's your job. It's how you stay in business so you can DO YOUR JOB and make a living doing it!

Yeah, yeah, yeah, whatever, Jennifer. Who cares? What's your point?

My point is that our clients deserve better. They just do.

Our buyers and sellers deserve our full attention. They deserve to be our top priority. And until we give them our full attention and make them our top priorities, we'll never enjoy the professional respect we so long for.

And as long as our industry considers our primary duty to be lead generation, **we won't deserve it**.

Conclusion

"Your work is not to drag the world kicking and screaming into a new awareness. Your job is to simply do your work...sacredly, secretly, and silently...and those with eyes to see and ears to hear will respond."
--The Arcturians

I wrote this book with the stated goal of inspiring like-minded real estate licensees to strive to be both Exceptional in the service they provide to their clients, and Professional in the manner in which they provide it.

And in an ideal world, every real estate licensee (and the brokers who manage them) would read this book, pump their fists in the air and declare: "THIS is how we shall run our businesses starting today!"

Sigh.

Ain't gonna happen.

Why on earth not? I mean, what can you possibly find to argue with in a business philosophy that encourages practitioners to be good at what they do and to behave professionally while doing it?

Well...

Do We Want to Change?

The first question to ask is—do we really care? Do we sincerely want to see a change in the industry or are we happy with our place in society?

The answer to this question very likely depends on how changing the industry would affect each of us. Would we make more money...or less? Would we have more flexibility...or less? Would we have more paperwork to process...or less? More training...or less? Would we make more money...or less? (Repeated intentionally.)

But for the sake of discussion, let's work under the assumption that we DO want to see our industry become more respected, more trusted and more positively perceived by the general public.

I'm not the first person to express a desire for this—far from it. For years, many within our ranks have been crying out for higher barriers to entry with proposals that include requiring a college degree, developing more intensive and relevant pre-license education and imposing tougher continuing education requirements.

All fine and good. Certainly raising the bar to entry would weed out a significant number of agents who simply see real estate as a get-rich-quick scheme. I'm in.

But it's not The Answer. It might be part of The Answer, but there's much more.

The problem seems to be one of motivation. Sure, we would like to be more trusted and respected by the general public, but not passionately enough to do much about it. Nothing, at least, beyond running expensive ads proclaiming our value and professionalism in hopes of revamping our image **from the outside in.**

But I believe, in order to effect meaningful change, that change needs to come from the **inside out**—that is, we need to change WHO WE ARE in order to convince the public that WE ARE that which we so long to be.

While I don't have all the answers, I believe there are two things we could do as an industry to effect the sweeping change I'm talking about. The first is easy. The second, not so.

Let's Start with Easy

What if the real estate regulatory community prohibited the title of "salesperson" (or any variation of) for a licensed real estate agent? Upon licensure, we could be real estate agents, real estate advisors, real estate professionals, real estate brokers, real estate associates, real estate consultants, real estate managers, or, here's a crazy one—real estate service managers?

Perhaps we could go a step further and prohibit the use of the word "salesperson" (or variations of) in all real estate-related personal marketing?

Just a thought. And I like it. A lot.

Onto the Not-So-Easy Path to Professionalism

Let's change WHO we attract into our industry and thus change our reputation from the inside out.

Currently, due to our compensation structure and the general perception that real estate is a sales profession, we attract, well, salespeople. People who were called to real estate, not because they are passionate about helping others achieve their dreams of home ownership, or even because they enjoy the process of putting and keeping buyers and sellers together, but because they enjoy the challenge of pursuing business. In other words, they are natural salespeople in search of a product to sell, and real estate sounds as good as any.

These natural salespeople enjoy nothing more than a good morning of cold-calling followed by an afternoon of belly-to-belly networking. Some even dismiss those pesky details of a real estate transaction as beneath them, worthy only of delegation to an administrative assistant or transaction coordinator (and yet proclaim that their ~~assistant's~~ services are worth thousands of dollars.)

But what if, instead of attracting salespeople-in-search-of-a-product-to-sell, we attracted people who have a natural passion and propensity for serving and taking care of the client? Client-centric, service-oriented **professionals** who have a sincere interest in creating happy experiences for their customers? People who enjoy (and are good at) managing the details of a real estate transaction, solving seemingly unsolvable problems and seeking a win/win solution for everyone involved whenever possible?

But Jennifer, we already have those people in real estate. They're our licensed assistants and transaction coordinators. Besides, service-oriented people aren't capable of bringing in business, so they'd certainly fail.

Well, first, if someone is capable of consistently seeing real estate transactions through from start to finish, they are far more than an assistant. Competently managing a real estate transaction involves more than document-shuffling and appointment-scheduling. If a real estate "assistant" is capable of successfully managing the entire process, then he is a partner, not an underling, and deserves to be acknowledged and compensated accordingly.

As far as bringing in business is concerned, every industry has this dilemma. In fact, real estate is a rather odd industry in that the "sales" force is also responsible for the subsequent servicing of the client. It really doesn't make sense if you think about it. Proficiency in sales and proficiency in service are two very different skill sets and it's unreasonable to expect anyone to be good at both.

Since we're working under the assumption that we are revamping the real estate industry business model, whatcha' think about a model where there is a small sales force or marketing department that is responsible for bringing business into the firm where it is then professionally and competently handled by people who are Exceptional managers of a real estate transaction?

But Jennifer, that'll never work because customer service people paid on a salary would never work as hard as they would if they were paid on commission!

... HA.

(That's me laughing snottily.)

Sorry, but I don't buy it. First, I don't believe that the majority of real estate agents are motivated to provide Exceptional customer service by the nature of their commission-based compensation structure. Oh, they're motivated all right, but in a different direction. They're motivated to prospect prospect prospect, chasing after that next commission check, not serve serve serve to ensure that their customer has a positive experience.

Second, who says salaried employees don't work hard? I don't know about you, but when I was in a professional salaried position prior to my venture into real estate, I worked damn hard, and I took pride in my work. I was well-paid to work damn hard, but that wasn't the deciding factor. I had a good work ethic and yes, I cared about my customers. Are nurses paid on commission? Teachers? Firefighters? Veterinarians? Paralegals?

And third, who's to say that a client-centric customer-service-dedicated real estate agent can't also be well-compensated on a pay-for-performance basis? Nothing in the business model I'm suggesting rules that out; we'd just need to figure out how to reconfigure the structure. We're smart people; I think we can come up with something ;-]

And finally, providing great service results in repeat and referral business. It just does. Give client-centric customer-service-oriented professionals the opportunity and support TO serve the customer Exceptionally well and those customers will be back and will send all their friends.

Frankly, I'm thinking the client-centric customer-service-oriented real estate professional could hire her own administrative assistant to do her marketing so she could focus on the **more important** job of taking care of her clients! After all, even with all the homage we pay to the unique value of the salesperson, an awful lot of real estate "sales" activity boils down to administrative tasks. Seriously—how much attention do we pay to our marketing calendars, magnets, newsletters and postcards? (A lot). To creating and maintaining a decent website? To writing coherent and appealing copy for brochures, newspaper ads and About Me's?

All of these activities can easily be handled by a reasonably intelligent, creative and tech-savvy assistant, freeing up the client-centric service-dedicated professional to focus on her current clients. To preparing for and going on listing appointments. To helping frustrated sellers figure out why their house hasn't sold. To staying on top of the ever-evolving market so that she can best help her buyers find and contract on their dream house. To DOING all those things a home buyer or seller expects her (and pays her) to be doing on their behalf.

But While We're on the Subject...How About a Salaried Real Estate Agent?

A few years ago, I posted a series of articles exploring the concept of a salaried real estate agent. The series got a lot of attention, but as expected, not a lot of support. The vast majority of followers commented that they hated the idea and many mentioned that they wouldn't have gone into real estate if they knew they'd be punching a clock, chained to a desk or accountable to an incompetent boss.

Fair enough. I don't much like the idea of clock-punching, desk-chaining or being accountable to an idiot either. And I like being paid on contingency; it suits my personality to be rewarded for working harder and/or smarter. But my question to the crowd wasn't whether or not THEY liked the idea for themselves; it was whether or not the notion had merit. But, alas, most readers couldn't get beyond what was "in it for me," which, sadly, perhaps made my point.

But the most common objection to the salaried real estate agent (and for simplicity, let's just call all non-contingency-based models "salaried") is that without the incentive to perform, service to the client would suffer.

In theory, that makes perfect sense; as I've experienced too many times, once you've paid for something, you're stuck with the service you get or don't get, whether you're satisfied or not satisfied.

But here's the thing. That blanket assumption actually contradicts a big part of the traditional real estate compensation model—specifically, that we are paid a percentage of the deal. That is—we usually make far more money on a $500,000 deal than on a $100,000 one. Therefore, the anti-salary line of reasoning implies that we will naturally work far harder on the bigger deal than on the smaller deal.

I don't know about you, but I don't work that way. My $100,000 clients got pretty much the same attention and service as my $500,000 ones. Not necessarily because it's the nice thing to do, but because that's who I am. If someone hires me to do a job for them and I agree to be hired by them, my pride ain't gonna allow me to give them a half-a$$ed effort, regardless of the final paycheck.

...ow I'm wired. Aren't you?

So, if we agree that we don't treat our lower dollar-versus-higher dollar clients much differently, is it really that big of a leap to assume that we are capable of providing excellent service under a salaried model?

If you were hired and paid a decent salary to take great care of a portfolio of buyers and sellers, would you really do a sub-standard job because **you aren't being paid on contingency**? Or would you take your job seriously and do your best because **that's who you are**?

> *From The Napoleon Hill Foundation*
>
> "Those who do no more than they are paid for have no real basis for requesting more pay because they are already getting all they deserve to earn.
>
> If you look around you, it will be apparent that there are two types of people in the world. There are those who say, "When this company decides to pay me what I'm worth, then I will do what they want me to do." The second is the person who says, "I'm going to be the best I can be because that's the kind of person I am. I also know that if I consistently give more than expected, I will eventually be rewarded for my efforts." It is easy to see that the positive person contributes most to the organization. Yet, very few people are willing to make the sacrifices necessary to achieve success. Make sure you're a member of that group."

There really isn't anything all that special about our industry that the business model used by most other industries couldn't possibly work for ours. And let's be honest, our industry isn't exactly setting the world on fire with the retention and success rates for our practitioners.

Before I went into real estate, I worked in the employee benefits sales department of a national health insurance carrier. Our office was staffed with sales reps and service reps. The sales reps did what you'd expect them to do—they lunched, schmoozed, networked, cold-called, warm-called, popped-by, mass-mailed, advertised, etc. We service reps managed the business the sales reps brought in—as soon as the ink was dry on the contracts, those clients belonged to us, and the sales rep moved on to the next prospect.

The system worked well. The salespeople made rain; the service people took (very good) care of the customer. We service reps didn't just work 9:00-5:00—it was in our job description to accommodate our clients even if that meant doing onsite employee meetings at 3:00am for the night shift. We had window offices, secretaries and expense accounts. We flew on corporate jets with our clients. Many of us had advanced industry-specific licenses. We were professionals.

But we weren't salespeople by any definition of the term. We serviced the business the sales force brought in and were well-trained (and well-paid) to do it. We were respected by the salespeople and by our clients (well, most of the time) and didn't consider ourselves glorified assistants. None of us (as I recall) had any desire to move into sales—we were perfectly happy and satisfied working our backsides off to fulfill the promises made by the rainmakers.

I can easily see a similar model where real estate agents are paid a good salary to do the job their buyers and sellers hire them to do. The companies that have the best tools, training and systems in place to serve their customers will naturally get a larger share of the local business, assuming they have a decent marketing department. Sure, there would be a sales force, but most real estate license-holders would focus on taking care of their current customers, rather than on the pursuit of new ones.

But Jennifer, other companies have tried that model and it didn't work. They went out of business!

Well, then they did something wrong, didn't they? Just because a few have tried and failed doesn't mean we should throw the whole concept out the window. Don't tell me it can't be done; companies in other industries do it every day.

And I'm thinking...if the owner of a salaried real estate company is going to invest in the tools, systems and training necessary to ensure his success and profitability, he might be a tad more interested and invested in what his troops are up to than your typical broker/owner is under the current model—y'think?

The fact is that what we have going right now ISN'T WORKING! Regardless of market conditions, the real estate industry has always "enjoyed" an enormous attrition (drop-out) rate, even during boom times. And last time I checked, the average income of a real estate agent hovered around $36,000, with an extremely low percentage earning over $100,000.

I repeat, what we're doing now is not working. Not for the client, not for the agent, and not for the broker owners. No one is winning. So, if it's broken...let's FIX it! Or at least be willing to think about fixing it.

Higher Barriers to Entry?

Let's return to something I mentioned in passing at the beginning of this Conclusion. The concept of imposing higher standards to obtain a real estate license. It's certainly worth considering, but would have to be done thoughtfully and strategically **with the end goal clearly in mind**.

Which is…? **I'm not sure**. Is the goal to create an industry with even more prolific rainmakers? Or to create an industry with better transaction managers?

Honestly, I'm asking. Because, again, the definition of success in a real estate career has always been based on production and lead generation, not on competent transaction management. So I'm not convinced that our industry as a whole actually **wants** to raise the bar on its members.

But just for fun, let's say that our industry decides to celebrate service-to-the-customer over bringing-new-customers-in-the-door. Let's imagine that we give ourselves the respect and dignity we demand from the public by attracting a higher-qualified practitioner and imposing much tougher entrance requirements.

For example, how about requiring at least an associate's degree prior to licensure? Doesn't have to be related to real estate, but at least it demonstrates a commitment to higher education.

And how about a longer, more intensive course of study to obtain a license? One that doesn't simply teach the pre-licensee how to pass the state exam, but actually how to manage the moving pieces and parts of a real estate transaction?

And, (here's my favorite part), what if we required the newly licensed real estate professional to work as an apprentice under an experienced mentor, one who is specifically trained TO train new agents? And is paid (by the new licensee) for the mentoring? And until the new licensee demonstrates a certain level of competence and expertise, he's not allowed to make a dime?

Do you think we'd weed out A LOT of poorly motivated, poorly funded and, frankly, marginally qualified real estate agents with this approach? Do you think we'd end up with a much smaller, yet far more capable community of real estate professionals?

Do you think we'd finally begin to enjoy the respect and admiration from the public we so long for…and, under this scenario, might actually deserve?

And the kicker—for the more mercenary among us (myself included)—less competition for our services and therefore more money in our pockets?

Oh, I hear the protests coming in already. *"But Jennifer, most agents would NEVER have gotten into real estate if they'd had to be that prepared ahead of time!"* *"But Jennifer, very few agents could afford to take six months off for schooling and another six months to work for free!"*

<u>My point exactly</u>.

But you know what? While more difficult, it's certainly not impossible or even unreasonable. College students do it every day. Medical students do it every day. Shoot, hairstylists and massage therapists do it every day! The person who does your nails probably had to invest more time and money into getting her cosmetology license than you did to get your real estate license.

~~~~~~~~~~~~~~~~~~~~~~~~~~~~~

Jennifer's Blog: "I'm Looking for a New Agent Training Program"

Every month or so I get a phone call from a managing broker wanting information on my "new agent training program." Within a matter of minutes, I can tell if the broker is a good prospect for my approach to rookie real estate agent training and the vast majority of the time, we part ways politely, never to speak again.

And I'm okay with that.

Here's how the conversation usually goes:

> **Caller:** "Hi, my name is Broker Bobby and I'm interested in your training program for new agents."
>
> **Jennifer:** "Wonderful! I'm so glad you called. Tell me more about what you're looking for."
>
> **Broker Bobby:** "Well, I need a training program for my new agents."
>
> **Jennifer:** "Okay, I have one of those. How much do you know about my approach to a real estate career?"
>
> **Broker Bobby:** (Laughs). "Not much, actually. I was just searching online for 'new real estate agent training' and found your website."
>
> **Jennifer:** (Laughs). "No problem. Let me tell you a little bit about my philosophies and see if you think it's a good fit for you. I believe that new licensees should spend their first 30 days focusing exclusively on learning their craft and that's what my rookie training program is all about. On becoming competent—learning their contracts, their systems and their market. I don't believe they should be encouraged, or shoot, even allowed to prospect for business until they have spent those 30 days, 8 hours a day immersed in a competence-based training program. Then, when they and their broker or trainer are comfortable the new agent is capable of managing a real estate transaction—or at least— knowledgeable enough to manage it with proper oversight, only then will they begin to go out looking for their first clients."
>
> **Broker Bobby:** "Oh."

The conversation typically ends shortly thereafter, although sometimes Broker Bobby protests that "a real estate agent wouldn't be happy under those conditions—he'll want to get right out there and prospect!" or "We want our new agents out there prospecting from Day One!" or "The best way for a new agent to learn is to be working with buyers and sellers as soon as possible."

I will confess, I sometimes get a little passive-aggressive here, innocently saying something like: "Well, it just doesn't make sense to me, on one hand, to say that a real estate agent's service is worth thousands of dollars, but on the other, to send a brand new agent out in the world with zero training. I mean, that's disrespectful to the value we bring to the table, isn't it? If what we do is so easy that someone without any training at all can do it?"

Eh, I never claimed to be a super salesperson.

~ ~

I believe that the profession (and I use that word intentionally) of being a real estate agent can and should be one that commands a similar respect, admiration and trust among the public that an accountant, a teacher or a nurse enjoys.

But unless and until we inside the real estate industry want this badly enough to make significant changes in who we attract, how we train them and how they are compensated, nothing will change. And we will continue to get exactly what we deserve.

Are you in?

Appendix

BONUS! Real Estate Consulting – What's It All About?

Transaction Checklists

    Buyer Under Contract Checklist

    Listing Under Contract Checklist

    Active Listing Checklist

Additional Resources

BONUS! Real Estate Consulting—What's It All About?

Real-estate Con-sult-ant: [rē' əl, e stā't, kən sult'nt]—noun

1. Offers objective counsel and advice to clients on matters related to real estate in which they have expertise.

2. Can provide a wide variety of real estate-related services, including but not limited to services related to buying or selling property.

3. Has the freedom and flexibility to charge for time spent, service provided and risk accepted as appropriate, which may include hourly rates, fee-for-service or -project, contingent fees, traditional commission or any combination of these.

As of this writing, real estate "consulting" has been slowly (very slooooowly) infiltrating the consciousness of the traditional real estate industry for about 15 years. In fact, the author of this book (that would be me) has had a small role in the infiltration after I took over the Accredited Consultant in Real Estate® (ACRE) designation program from ACRE founder Mollie Wasserman in 2011.

While real estate consulting has a long way to go before it can be considered remotely mainstream in the real estate industry, the basic premises and philosophies of consulting fit in quite nicely with being an Exceptional real estate Professional. So I hope you enjoy this little bonus section on what real estate consulting is all about.

A Real Estate Consultant (as we define it around here) is a real estate practitioner who believes in offering real estate consumers transparent CHOICES when it comes to the services they receive and how they pay for those services. A Real Estate Consultant recognizes that the traditional real estate compensation structure of being paid a contingent fee based on the sales price of the product they "sell" does not always serve the best interests of the buyer or seller, nor, for that matter, the best interests of the real estate practitioner.

A Real Estate Consultant also realizes that not all real estate consumers need (or want to pay for) the "full package" of services that our industry typically offers, and therefore the consultant offers alternative products and services to better fit the needs of each individual client. And finally, because a Real Estate Consultant has the desire and ability to customize his (or her) offerings and fees, he (or she) enjoys far more opportunities to serve the real estate needs of the consumers in his (or her) community!

More Services + More Potential Clients = More Income Potential!

And of course, as the title "consultant" implies, a real estate consultant considers himself to be an advisor to his clients, not a salesperson to his clients.

There's more, so much more, but that's the gist of it. If it sounds intriguing to you, here is a little quiz to help you decide if real estate consulting is right for you at this point in your career.

Is Real Estate Consulting Right For You? A Quiz to Find Out!

Each of the following questions present a statement and asks if you agree or disagree with it. There are no right or wrong answers, per se; however, the "correct" answer shown reflects the attitude a consulting-minded real estate professional would have on the matter. If you find that you agree with most of the "correct" answers given, then you'll probably enjoy the ACRE approach to real estate. If you find that you disagree with most of the "correct" answers, that's okay, too!

Question One
"I love the thrill of working on commission and feel I'd be leaving money on the table working under any other compensation model."

A) I disagree with this statement. I can see many benefits to working under a compensation model that is not based solely on being paid by commission.

B) I agree with this statement. Working by commission guarantees me the highest possible paycheck and is a lot more fun than being paid by the hour or by the project.

Correct Answer: A
Hey, we understand the thrill of working by commission and there's nothing quite like leaving the closing table with a $5,000, $10,000 or even $20,000 check! And yes, the uncertain nature of our compensation IS something that many of us thrive on.

We get that.

However, when real estate practitioners balk at the notion of charging fees (as opposed to commissions) due to their belief that they'll be leaving money on the table, they're really comparing apples and pomegranates.

When you are paid by a contingent commission (the traditional model), your paycheck includes a significant risk mitigation factor. So, for example, if you receive a commission check of $6,000 at closing, at least half (maybe more) of that figure is "earned" by your accepting the risk of not being paid at all (if the transaction never closes). Risk = Reward. Higher Risk = Higher Reward.

However, when you work on a fee basis, your risk is partially or completely eliminated. The same transaction that paid you $6,000 under the traditional model might pay you "only" $2,500 under a fee arrangement, but that $2,500 is guaranteed (depending on how you set up your fees).

And here's an interesting twist—you can offer your client the OPTION to pay you either contingently or non-contingently, explaining that your fee is less when you're paid non-contingently because you're taking less risk. You don't have to decide for him or her; one of the cornerstones of a good consulting model is offering your clients intelligent, transparent choices in how they compensate you.

Imagine if every buyer you worked with last year (not just the ones who went to a closing) paid you a fee upfront in exchange for a full or partial rebate of your commission at the closing...and if there was no closing, you retained the payment. Imagine if every seller paid a non-refundable upfront fee in exchange for a lower listing commission...and if the home didn't sell, you kept that fee.

If you do the math, **including all the buyers and sellers you worked with who never made it to the closing table**, you'll probably see that you wouldn't have left any money on the table and might have even come away with more!

Obviously, there's more to the story than these simple examples, but don't just assume that because you receive less money per transaction that you're leaving money on the table when charging on a fee basis.

Question Two
"I struggle to explain to my higher-end clients why they pay so much more for my service than my lower-end clients pay."

A) I disagree with this statement. It all evens out in the end—the higher fees my upper-end clients pay offset the fees my lower-end clients pay, so in the end, I'm fairly compensated for my work.

B) I agree with this statement. It doesn't seem fair to my clients buying or selling more expensive properties to charge them more just to make up for the lower fees I receive when working with clients buying or selling lower priced properties.

Correct Answer: B
"It all evens out in the end" may very well be true for the real estate licensee, but it's not at all fair to the clients who pay more than their share to make up for the lower commissions collected on smaller transactions.

We believe that every client should be charged an appropriate amount for his or her individual transaction, not be asked to subsidize transactions where the real estate practitioner does not charge enough to fairly compensate him or herself. And yes, this may mean that you charge **more** (as a percentage of the property's price) for less expensive properties and **less** for more expensive properties. It might also mean that your pricing is not competitive on lower-priced properties and that's a business decision you'll have to make for yourself.

Question Three
"I sometimes wonder why a buyer or seller would trust my advice, given that my compensation is determined by the decisions they make, based in whole or in part on the advice I give."

A) I agree with this statement. If I were hiring someone to represent my best interests, but they only got paid if I bought something, I'd certainly wonder where their true interest lies.

B) I disagree with this statement. If my client doesn't trust me, then they can find another agent to work with.

Correct Answer: A
Now THIS is the elephant in the room that SHOULD make every real estate licensee pause and wonder why on earth our compensation model is the way it is. The way we are compensated (under the traditional model) creates an inherent conflict of interest between our living up to our fiduciary duties (which we agree to when we accept agency) and our being paid for our work. And we wonder why the general public doesn't trust us; why they named us as the

second LEAST trusted profession in a 2008 survey (we were second only to stockbrokers).

If your clients DO trust that you have their best interests at heart, then you are to be congratulated...because you have earned that trust IN SPITE of the way we're paid, not because of it.

Question Four
"My managing broker will never in a million years let me charge clients upfront and I'm not willing to change offices."

A) I agree with this statement. There's no point in even asking; my broker is dead-set against charging less than X% commission and I don't feel like changing offices right now.

B) I disagree with this statement. If I approach my broker with a well-thought-out plan to incorporate consulting, he or she might just go for it. If not, I am willing to change offices because I believe real estate consulting is the right approach for me.

Correct Answer: B
It's quite possible that your managing broker will not see the value in adding real estate consulting to the office business model, especially if you work in a large national franchise. However, don't automatically assume this to be so; give your broker the benefit of the doubt and assume that if YOU see the wisdom in real estate consulting, he or she might as well.

That said, you MUST be fully prepared to explain to your broker what real estate consulting is...and is not...and show him or her your plan to make it work in your business. If you just refer your broker to the ACRE website and hope that will do the trick, it probably won't.

If you truly believe there is no place for real estate consulting in your office and you are committed to being a real estate consultant, you will need to go elsewhere. And yes, there probably are real estate companies in your market place who will let you run your business the way you see fit.

Question Five
"I like the idea of real estate consulting, but there's no way it will work in my market."

A) I agree. No way anyone is going to pay upfront for services they can get for free from the guy down the block. There's just too much competition here.

B) I disagree. I believe that real estate consulting, when practiced properly is a win/win for both me and the consumer; therefore it most certainly will work in my market.

Correct Answer: B
We hear this every day: "Sounds good, but it'll never work."

But that's not true. It can work and it does work; just ask our practicing ACREs. The confusion lies in a misperception of WHAT real estate consulting really is. Many believe that consulting is simply a gimmick to "force" the consumer to pay us upfront, with no real benefit to the client of doing so, and if that were the case, then, no, it probably won't work.

But when practiced properly, real estate consulting truly creates a win/win for both parties—the consultant AND the client. We don't ask anyone to try to "sell" anything they wouldn't "buy" themselves, and that includes real estate consulting services. Consultants offer intelligent, transparent choices to their clients in the services they receive and how they pay for those services and let them choose which solution is best for them.

How can anyone argue with that?

Question Six
"I don't know how I'll possibly convince my clients that consulting is of benefit to them."

A) I disagree with this statement. Real estate consulting is all about giving the consumer what they want and need, and charging a fair price for it. And as long as what I offer IS of benefit to the consumer (not just to me), "convincing" them will be a non-issue.

B) I agree with this statement. People are used to paying by commission and that's the way it will always be.

Correct Answer: A
We discussed this in the last question, but we'll continue it a bit further. There should never be a need to "convince" anyone that professional real estate consulting is right for them because the whole point of being a consultant is to help your client determine the best solution(s) for their situation. When you act

as a consultant, you don't do so in hopes of forcing the client or prospect into the solution (and payment plan) YOU prefer; you are simply providing objective counsel on a subject in which you have expertise. Therefore, no "convincing" should be required or even attempted.

And again...who could argue with that?

Question Seven
"When I meet with a buyer prospect for the first time, my goal is to convince him that now is the right time to buy."

A) I disagree. When I meet with a buyer, my goal is to help him determine if now is the right time for him to buy, given his individual situation and goals.

B) I agree with this statement. If a buyer doesn't buy, I don't get paid, so obviously I'm going to push him to buy sooner than later!

Correct Answer: A
Pushing a potential buyer to BUY NOW will, in most cases, result in the potential buyer wondering where your interests lie and if you're really looking out for his best interests. Even if now IS a great time for him to buy, if he feels pressure from you, he won't be comfortable with that, or with you.

A consultant's approach is to help the potential buyer evaluate his personal situation, the current state of the market and his goals and reach the right decision for him.

What's Next?

Whew. That's a lot to think about. But we're guessing that it either makes perfect sense to you...or it doesn't.

If it does make sense to you, please visit the ACRE website at **www.TheConsultingProfessional.com**. We'd love to have you join us!

Additional SWS Resources

More Books by Jennifer Allan-Hagedorn

Sell with Soul: Creating an Extraordinary Career in Real Estate without Losing Your Friends, Your Principles or Your Self-Respect

The More Fun You Have Selling Real Estate, the More Real Estate You Will Sell

Prospect with Soul: Discovering the Perfect Prospecting Strategies for Wonderful, Extraordinary, One-of-a-Kind YOU

Selling Real Estate without Selling Your Soul, Volume 1

Selling Real Estate without Selling Your Soul, Volume 2

It Really Is That Simple

Learn more and purchase at the SWS Bookstore - **www.SWSStore.com**

SWS Courses & Programs

The Exceptional Agent Program: Because Competence Gives You Confidence

SOI with SOUL: Building a Sphere of Influence Business Model from Scratch—No Referral-Begging or Pestering Required!

The SWS School for Rookie Real Estate Agents

Selling with Soul for Life: Seven Weeks of Building Your Business...for Life!

The Accredited Consultant in Real Estate® Course and Designation

Learn more and purchase at the SWS Bookstore - **www.SWSStore.com**

The SWS Community

Club SWS - **www.ClubSWS.Info**

SWS Connect - **www.SWSConnect.com**

The Accredited Consultant in Real Estate® - **www.TheConsultingProfessional.com**

The Searchable Soul Blog Archive - **www.SearchableSoul.com**

Sample Listing-Under-Contract Checklist

As contract-to-closing protocol varies significantly by market area, be sure to confirm the accuracy and appropriateness of each item in your specific jurisdiction.

Activity	Due Date	√ When Complete
Get the earnest money check	Day of Contract	
Turn in contract file to office manager	Day of Contract	
Enter contract dates into your contract manager program	Day of Contract	
Order title work and HOA documents	Day of Contract	
Change the status in the MLS	Day of Contract	
Notify showing desk/showing service of status change	Day of Contract	
Notify agents with showing appointments of status change	Day of Contract	
Send property disclosures to the buyer agent	Day of Contract	
Call buyer's lender and introduce yourself	1st Week after Contract	
Pick up the brochure box	1st Week after Contract	
Get payoff information from seller	1st Week after Contract	
Property disclosures returned from buyer with signature?	1st Week after Contract	
Put up SOLD sign	2nd Week after Contract	
Call buyer's lender	2nd Week after Contract	
Prepare for the appraisal	2nd Week after Contract	
Set the closing	2nd Week after Contract	
Confirm that the inspection items are complete	1 Week before Closing	
Confirm that seller has arranged cleaning	1 Week before Closing	
Arrange mail-out close or POA	1 Week before Closing	
Send any changes to lender and/or title company	1 Week before Closing	
Is the buyer doing a walk-thru?	1 Week before Closing	
Confirm closing time, date & place with all parties	1 Week before Closing	
Review closing figures	1-2 Days before Closing	
Remind seller to bring driver's license to closing	1-2 Days before Closing	
Order earnest money check from office manager	1-2 Days before Closing	
Prepare the file for closing	1-2 Days before Closing	
Pick up the sign, lockbox and interior brochure box	Day of Closing	
Turn in closed file to office manager	Right after Closing	
Notify showing desk/showing service of closed status	Right after Closing	
Add seller to post-closing follow-up plan	1-2 Days after Closing	
Update seller's address in your Contact Manager	1-2 Days after Closing	
Call seller after move-out	3-5 Days after Closing	
Update websites with sale	3-5 Days after Closing	

Sample Active Listing Checklist

Activity	Due Date	√ When Complete
Seller signature on all listing contracts & disclosures	Prior to MLS entry	
Take pictures	Prior to MLS entry	
Schedule/create the Virtual Tour	Prior to MLS entry	
Get the key, install the lockbox	Prior to MLS entry	
Get HOA contact information from seller	Prior to MLS entry	
Install the For Sale sign	Day of MLS entry	
Enter the listing on MLS	Day of MLS entry	
Enter the listing on your contact manager program	Day of MLS entry	
Order 'Just Listed' cards	Day of MLS entry	
Track the expiration date	Day of MLS entry	
Turn in file to office	Day of MLS entry	
Send showing instructions to showing desk/showing service	Day of MLS entry	
Create & display 'Special Features' cards in the home	Day of MLS entry	
Send a copy of the MLS listing to the seller	Day of MLS entry	
Deliver copies of all signed documents to seller	1 Day after MLS entry	
Prepare the home brochure	1 Day after MLS entry	
Schedule open house/put up Open Sunday sign rider	1 Day after MLS entry	
Call the HOA to verify information	Within 1st week	
Deliver home brochures to home	When ready	
Solicit feedback, provide to seller	1st week after MLS entry	(Ongoing)
Load Internet advertising	1st week after MLS entry	
Email web links of advertising to seller	1st week after MLS entry	
Fluff & Flush 1	7 Days after MLS entry	
First market report to seller	7 Days after MLS entry	
Call seller "Are the showing instructions working for you?"	7 Days after MLS entry	
Preview new competing listings/report findings to seller	2nd week after MLS entry	
Fluff & Flush 2	2nd week after MLS entry	
Call seller "Need more brochures yet?"	2nd week after MLS entry	
Fluff & Flush 3 (continue every week)	3rd week after MLS entry	
Call seller to check in	3rd week after MLS entry	
Second market report to seller	3rd week after MLS entry	
Preview new competing listings/report findings to seller	4th week after MLS entry	
Prepare & schedule 6-week CMA meeting/3rd market update	6th week after MLS entry	
Pick up brochure box	6th week after MLS entry	
Re-do exterior photos?	When season changes	
Fourth market update to seller	8th week after MLS entry	

Sample Buyer-Under-Contract Checklist

As contract-to-closing protocol varies significantly by market area, be sure to confirm the accuracy and appropriateness of each item in your jurisdiction.

Activity	Due Date	√ When Complete
Enter contract dates into contact management program	Day of Contract	
Send contract to lender	Day of Contract	
Deliver property disclosures to buyer	Day of Contract	
Deliver earnest money to listing agent	Day of Contract	
Give buyer HOA contact information & questionnaire	Day of Contract	
Give buyer inspector names & numbers	Day of Contract	
Call buyer's lender to confirm loan application	1st Week after Contract	
Call buyer's lender to discuss scheduling appraisal	1st Week after Contract	
Deliver signed disclosures to listing agent	1st Week after Contract	
Tell buyer to look into homeowner hazard insurance	1st Week after Contract	
Call buyer's lender to check in	1st Week after Contract	
Has closing been scheduled?	1st Week after Contract	
Is buyer doing a mail-out close or POA?	2nd Week after Contract	
Are the inspection items done?	1 Week before Closing	
Get documentation of inspection repairs	1 Week before Closing	
Schedule walk-thru	1 Week before Closing	
Remind buyer to transfer utilities	1 Week before Closing	
Send any changes to lender and/or title company	2-4 Days before Closing	
Confirm closing time & place	2-4 Days before Closing	
Review closing figures with buyer	2-4 Days before Closing	
Tell buyer to bring driver's license & cashier's check to closing	2-4 Days before Closing	
Prepare the file for closing	Right before Closing	
Turn the file in to the office manager	Right after Closing	
Add buyer to your SOI (or change buyer's address)	Right after Closing	
Add buyer to your post-closing follow-up program	Right after Closing	
Call buyer to check on move	4 Days after Closing	